Language and Religious Language

Westminster Studies in Christian Communication

Kendig Brubaker Cully, General Editor

Language
and Religious
Language

A Study in the Dynamics of Translation

JULES LAURENCE MOREAU

THE WESTMINSTER PRESS

Philadelphia

COPYRIGHT © MCMLXI W. L. JENKINS

LIBRARY OF CONGRESS CATALOG CARD NO. 60–10170

To

MARY ELIZABETH

whose devoted patience
and

ALDEN DREW

*whose continued encouragement
converge toward a definition of*
agapē

Contents

A Note on Westminster Studies
in Christian Communication

These Studies, for which the first two volumes are foundational, are predicated on the ground that the Christian faith needs to be made relevant to persons in the modern world in terms of the dynamic nature of the faith itself and the channels that are capable of conveying such a faith. In itself any technique of communication conceivably could serve as well for secular as for religious ends. In this series a wide variety of means and methods of communication will be analyzed in the light of their availability to, and suitability for, the particular tasks that the Christian church faces in bringing the realities of faith to bear upon the life of actual persons in the contemporary situation.

Oftentimes in the past, techniques have been viewed almost as ends in themselves. Or, they have been taken over uncritically from the secular culture without being subjected to adequate scrutiny as to whether they are appropriate for the church's use. On the other hand, sometimes the church has been blind to the life situations of the present to such an extent as to ignore the real ways in which people's lives are influenced by all that impinges on them. In the latter case, the church has failed to bring the life-giving power of the gospel to bear on contemporary culture because of a lack of understanding of, or appreciation for, the means of communication that have been proved capable of changing lives and societies.

Involving as it does both the "What" and the "How," the whole question of the communication of the gospel in the modern world is pivotal in the present juncture of history. Starting with these initial volumes, the present Studies will be aimed at bringing the "What" and the "How" together fruitfully. These books are designed to make a contribution to the ongoing conversations across boundaries. Theology, Biblical studies, sociology, cultural anthropology, psychology, education, art, letters, science, and the other disciplines, all have something to say to one another. In our present concern, " communication " refers to the way in which the Christian faith can come into conjunction with what is happening in the total world of life and ideas in the middle decades of the twentieth century. In each of these Studies attention will focus on some important aspect of the basic question: How can the church most effectively preach, teach, and otherwise manifest the gospel in the growing edges of man's present-day culture? No aspect of man's actual situation is alien to such a question. No medium of communication should fail to come under scrutiny if, as Christians, we are eager to have the Word of God confront a confused generation powerfully and compellingly.

Each volume in Westminster Studies in Christian Communication will be an authentic voice of one perceptive interpreter. No effort has been made to suggest to any writer what " line " he ought to follow. Each work will be adjudged by the readers on its own merits. The writers themselves conceivably might disagree heartily with regard to certain presuppositions or conclusions held by their colleagues. All this will be to the good if the result of these Studies should be the stimulating of many conversations. Yet all the writers have in mind a focus that is realistic, an emphasis that is practical, and a discussion that is timely. The only request made of the authors is that they speak out of their knowledge to the very heart and mind of our times. Depth without dullness, breadth without diffuseness, challenge without sentimentality — these, at least, it is hoped, will be characteristic of all the Studies. We are grateful to those who have consented to share in this venture into communication, and we commend their work as in itself an integral part of the church's task of communication.

KENDIG BRUBAKER CULLY
General Editor

Evanston, Illinois

Preface

More than a dozen years devoted to teaching the language and literature of the New Testament only increases our conviction that the degree to which a student succeeds in penetrating the Biblical structure of meaning will determine his adequacy as an interpreter of the Christian faith. Far too few theological students have the tools or the motivation to work effectively at gaining an appreciation of this meaning structure. In part, this lack is due to an antiquated method of language teaching, but it also stems from the fragmented view of theological study that underlies the curriculum of the vast majority of theological schools; it is further compounded by the pedagogical stance of most theological faculties. Ministers who have been educated in these institutions pass their confusion on to the church, with the result that the average layman is so frustrated in his attempt to understand the Christian faith that he is content to leave theology to the experts.

Whether we like it or not, a theology will emerge whenever two or more people discuss the Christian faith even in its most elementary terms. The language employed to discuss the Christian faith is theological language; as such, it carries a theology. The question, then, is not, "Shall we have theology?" Instead, it is, "What theology do we have?" The present study is an attempt to examine this question descriptively and historically. On this basis, it would point out the direction to be taken by a church responsive both to its own history and to the present situation.

As we have seen it, the mission of the church is to translate. The church cannot translate, however, until it has made certain both of *what* it is translating and of the environment *to which* it must translate. If the conception of the ministry of translation set forth in this book causes the church to ask again and attempt to answer anew some basic questions, it will have served its purpose in fostering communication.

JULES LAURENCE MOREAU

Evanston, Illinois

Chapter I

Christian Language in Perspective

The casual observer at a United Nations session is struck by the apparent ease with which negotiations are carried on despite the vastly different languages spoken by the participants. The delegates from the Soviet Union make their addresses, and after a translation of that address, the British, American, or French delegate replies. The same procedure is followed as each delegate speaks in his own native tongue or in one of the acknowledged diplomatic languages. Occasionally a diplomat is sufficiently familiar with the tongue of the representative of another nation to speak in that nation's tongue. It is rare, however, for a diplomatic conversation to be carried on in only one language, except when the conference involves two highly placed representatives of nations that have a common tongue.

Because the vocabulary of one tongue does not always fit neatly and exactly when translated into another tongue, misunderstandings often bar full communication between speakers of two different tongues. In the recent exchanges between nations within the orbit of the Soviet Union and members of the North Atlantic Treaty Organization, many such misunderstandings have been experienced. When a Soviet representative uses the words "freedom" and "democracy," it is evident to all the hearers that he does not mean precisely what a French, British, or German representative means by these words. Some of the difference in meaning is attributable to an

13

intention on the part of the participants in the conversation to confound each other. Regardless of how deep this intention may be, there is still a great deal of the difference that belongs to the peculiarity of the structure of a given language. Much of this structural peculiarity has to do with the way in which words are used in one language or another.

Just as our diplomats are at a distinct disadvantage if they do not understand the tongue of those with whom they must deal on the international scene, so are Christians at a disadvantage when they try to converse across the lines that have come to separate various provinces and denominations of the one church. Every meeting of the World Council of Churches poses this kind of problem. To overcome some of the more obvious difficulties, a translation service similar to that employed at the United Nations was in use during the Assembly at Evanston in 1954. Still, among vast numbers of those present it was impossible to secure any amount of verbal communication.

Some of the language barrier is overcome among Christians of the same denominational group in spite of their language differences. Swedish, German, Finnish, and American Lutheran groups have maintained enough similarity in their liturgical practices, so that they can worship together. Other groups of Christians who have kept the ancient liturgical structure, like the Anglicans or the various autocephalous churches of the East, can experience the same sort of non-linguistic communication because they can participate in a liturgical observance that transcends the barrier created by their now divergent national tongues. For groups whose liturgy is more fluid, flexible, and considerably less subject to formal and traditional patterns than those groups which we have already mentioned, this channel is closed except for those more or less universal expressions such as hymnody and psalmody. The result of common participation in a liturgy by Christians whose own traditions have maintained the traditional forms has been that they experience a sense of solidarity mediated by a nonlinguistic symbol. In order to articulate this experience, each national group would have to resort to its own language, but the articulation of the experience follows upon their sharing something with their brethren.

The point during the Evanston Assembly at which the language problem became most acute was in the discussion groups that met to consider the papers and addresses that had been previously prepared by some of the leading theologians of the World Council. Here the linguistic mode of communication was paramount, and here the problems began to appear in profusion. When an address was rendered from German into English, for example, the fine nuances intended by the speaker were frequently lost simply because the theological vocabulary of the German language carries with it a certain train of historical meaning which the equivalent words in English do not bear. Not seldom, in place of the intended nuances, a new set of peripheral notions entered the context because of the peculiar sense of the words chosen by English interpreters.

We can offer a relatively simple instance of this conditioned meaning of words by choosing a central term in the Christian vocabulary — "salvation." In English this word is closely associated with the idea of being saved. Through its Late Latin ancestor it also acquired a meaning closely related to the word "salvage." The notion inherent in the English word "salvation" has to do with rescuing something or someone from untoward circumstances or dire consequences. In its very narrow religious sense, the word preserves an important dimension of the gospel proclamation. Nevertheless, the overtones of the word are what one hears more loudly, and a certain image is created in the minds of the hearers. On the other hand, the German language employs for this notion a word derived from the same complex of terms as that which gives us our English word "heal." The emphasis in this word group is upon "making whole," and the consequent train of ideas motivated by this word is entirely different from that involved in "salvation." Hence, when a translator renders the German term *Heil* by the English word "salvation," something more than the mere substitution of an equivalent term has taken place.

The problem of translation from German into English is a relatively simple one because the two languages have a common background in the Teutonic family of languages. Part of the difficulty encountered in the translation of religious and theological material from German into English arises from the fact that English has a considerable vocabulary which is traceable to Late Latin. Because the English Church was so closely related to the Latin Church for almost a thousand years, much of the *theological* and *philosophical* vocabulary of English is of Latin origin. The theological and philosophical vocabulary of German is, on the contrary, what we call noncognate. That is to say, while English uses Latin terms in this context, German employs Teutonic terms. A simple example of this characteristic can be found in the terms employed by each of the languages for that branch of philosophy dealing with the theory of knowledge — how we know things. German uses *Erkenntnislehre*, which comes from two separate Teutonic words, *erkennen* (recognize or discern) and *lehren* (teach); English uses the word "epistemology," which can trace its ancestry through the Romanic languages back to Late Latin and ultimately to Greek. Modern English speech is recapturing some of the directness of Germanic expression, but in the realm of philosophy and theology the language cannot escape its historical association with the scholarship of the Latin-speaking medieval world.

If we are dismayed by the disparities caused by the store of Latin words in the English language, we ought to recall that whether Russian, German, English, French, or Greek, these languages all belong to a larger family of languages known as Indo-European or Indo-Aryan. That fact was demonstrated long ago by comparative philologists who traced root forms through language groups back to a common ancestor that they called Proto-Indo-European (PIE). This explains why we find it rather easier to learn German or even Russian than Chinese or some American Indian tongue. The language similarity existing among the various Indo-European tongues also implies that the speakers of these languages are concerned with somewhat similar basic problems of life. As a reflection of cultural development, language often provides a far better index of the basic problems with which that culture is concerned than some of the more articulate formulations of those problems. Languages have a strange way of sublimating problems in the levels of language with which its speakers are less familiar simply because they are infrequently conscious of the structure of their own language.

The translation problem is compounded many times over when we attempt to render into one of our Indo-European tongues the discourse of speakers of a language that is not within the Indo-European group. This fact becomes evident at once to a traveler in the Middle East. He may know all or most of the languages spoken on the northern shores of the Mediterranean Sea, but once he crosses to the southern shores or travels to the eastern end of the Mediterranean, he finds that Arabic is almost a necessity. When he begins to learn Arabic, however, he enters an entirely new thought world. What he can say in Greek or in some other European language, he is not always able to say in Arabic; and the reverse is true, for Arabic has its peculiar richness also. What he can say in Arabic he could probably repeat much more easily in Syriac or in Ivrit (modern Hebrew).

A. From Hebrew to Greek

If we were to share the experience of our Mediterranean voyager, we should experience in reverse what the Jewish community went through when it was scattered abroad from its homeland several centuries before our era. Forced to learn Greek in order to carry on business in the Hellenistic world, the Jews gradually lost contact with their native Semitic tongue and retained what bonds they had with it by means of regular synagogue worship. Thrust into a foreign environment, these Jews had to learn a tongue that was totally different from their own. The process was costly to the Jews, since they lost their all-important linguistic tie with the Palestinian homeland, but it was valuable to the Hellenistic world into which they were thrust. How valuable for the Western world this experience of the Jews was can be seen in the course of events during the first few centuries of our era.

Unlike many other cultural or national groups in the Hellenistic world, the Jews maintained a solidarity that resisted forces working toward assimilating them into general Hellenistic culture. What kept the community together was its religion. Not only were the Jews a "people of the Book" who gathered each Sabbath for a religious observance that centered upon reading and exposition of their sacred scriptures; they also bore the cultic mark of circumcision and observed quite rigid dietary prescriptions. Their cultic observances, such as refraining from work on the Sabbath, circumcising male babies, and refusing to eat certain foods, were the liturgical manifestation of a community conviction that it was an "elect people," the *populus Dei*. Their sacred scriptures told the story of their election to serve the God of Israel, Yahweh, and these scriptures were read in course in their regular synagogue services.

It is quite probable that the earliest Jews who were dispersed into the Hellenistic world were bilingual. Maintaining their native Semitic tongue, the pioneers of the Diaspora (the "dispersion") soon found it necessary to acquire more than minimal proficiency in the Hellenistic Greek that was the lingua franca of the regions which came under the hegemony of Alexander the Great (d. 323 B.C.) and his successors. After the death of Alexander, these vast regions were divided among the Ptolemies who governed Egypt, the Seleucids who ruled Syria including Palestine (for a considerable period, at least), and the Antigonids who, after much conflict, achieved control of Macedon on the European mainland. The language of the entire Mediterranean basin as well as many lands that stretched far inland was therefore Greek, and no business or other relations could be carried on without a knowledge of this language. Second and third generation Jews of the Diaspora may have remained bilingual, but during the second century before our era it seems clear that if a Jew in the Hellenistic world was able to speak and understand two languages, his Greek was obviously his first language.

The loyalties of the dispersed Jewish community were oriented to the Holy City, Jerusalem, and its Temple. If any Jew of the Diaspora ever realized his life ambition to make a pilgrimage to Jerusalem at Passover, the ritual which he attended would have been inspiring to him, but the language in which it was conducted would have been strange to him, if not altogether incomprehensible. This was so because a whole structure of Greek Judaism had emerged in the Diaspora. These dispersed Jews knew their sacred scriptures only in translation, and this fact could hardly fail to affect their religious outlook in a profound way. Consequently, these Jews were aware of their own sacred history in much the same way as many modern Christian communities who know their sacred scriptures only in the Authorized Version. Just as these modern Christian communities must depend upon a sixteenth century idiom for their religious vocabulary, so the Jews of the Diaspora were dependent for theirs upon a Hellenistic idiom of the third century before our era.

The custom of regular Sabbath worship, in which the reading of sacred scripture occupied a central position, brought about this Greek Judaism of the Diaspora. The Sabbath service consisted of readings from the Prophets (*Haftorah*) and from the Law (Pentateuch), some psalmody, a form of prayer, and an exposition of the text. In Palestine, the text of the scriptures was probably read, or more properly sung, in Hebrew; at the earlier stages of Judaism of the Diaspora, the same was probably true there also. As the Hebrew language became less the language spoken among the people in Palestine and thus became a " classical " language, it became necessary for a learned man to translate the sacred text after it was read into the spoken language. In Palestine, this meant that the Hebrew scriptures were translated after reading into Aramaic, the lingua franca of the Persian Empire. In the Hellenistic world, the translation had to be made into Greek. At first, no doubt, these translations were made freely during the synagogue service by men who were adequately familiar with both Hebrew and Greek. As the Judaism of the Diaspora lost active contact with Hebrew, however, there arose the need for a quasi-official translation of the Hebrew scriptures to be used in these services. This was the genesis of the Greek version of the Old Testament, which was ultimately known as the Septuagint (LXX). In Palestine, of course, the vernacular version took longer to reach written form since the language similarities were such that the rabbis would have no trouble in handling the translation; Hebrew remained a tongue known to the rabbis, just as our teachers of Bible know both Greek and Hebrew.

The precise history of the Greek version of the Old Testament is not easy to trace because of the complexities of Greek Judaism itself. Scholars are not unanimous about the manner in which the early translation was made, by whom, and where. One thing does seem certain, however, about the translation; several versions were reduced to writing, and this seems to imply that the history of the Septuagint is not completely dissimilar to the Aramaic translations (called Targums). A decided effort was made from Alexandria in the early part of the first century B.C. to commend, and possibly to enforce, a specific Greek version of the Pentateuch as both official and divinely inspired. Our evidence for this campaign is a letter written about 100 B.C. by an Alexandrian Jew and purporting to be from the hand of one Aristeas, an official in the Egyptian court of Ptolemy (II) Philadelphus (285–245 B.C.), to his brother Philocrates. This Letter of Aristeas relates a tale of how the Greek version was made. According to it, at the request of the librarian at Alexandria, Demetrius of Phaleron (d. ca. 283 B.C.), a mission was sent to Jerusalem by Ptolemy for the purpose of getting translators who would render the

Pentateuch into Greek for inclusion in the famous library and museum at Alexandria.

As the story goes, seventy-two elders were sent to Egypt from Palestine, rendered the Pentateuch on the island of Pharos in seventy-two days, and after being treated royally were sent back to their Palestinian home. In the course of telling his story, the author of this letter takes every opportunity to commend Judaism to Greeks, defend it against its derogators, and convey the impression that the excellencies of Judaism were appreciated by Ptolemy as well as by some of his closest associates. The particular part of the letter which directly involves the translation (pars. 301-317) is an eloquent defense of the Alexandrian version of the Pentateuch and gives rise to the name Septuagint (from the Latin word for " seventy ") by which the Greek version of the entire Old Testament came to be known commonly.

While the Alexandrian version of the Pentateuch may have overcome its rivals successfully to become the accepted version of these books in Greek Judaism, the case is somewhat different for the remaining books of the Old Testament. So far as we are able to ascertain, Hellenistic Judaism disappeared in the wake of the Christian gospel's invasion of this region before a similar standardization could be achieved for the Prophets and the Writings. At least two recensions are extant for some of the books, such as Judges and Daniel, while many differences from the standard Hebrew text (the Masoretic text) are to be found in such books as Samuel, Kings, and Jeremiah. Many of the books extant in the Greek also have no counterpart in the Hebrew canon of scripture; these books are represented in the Authorized Version by what we call the Apocrypha. Some of these books may have been composed in Greek by and for Hellenistic Jews, as, for example, the Second Book of Maccabees or certain parts of the Wisdom of Solomon. In any event, it seems that Hellenistic Judaism never had a standard Greek text of the Old Testament beyond the Pentateuch, nor did it establish specific boundaries as to what its scriptures should contain. Hence, when we speak of the Greek Old Testament, we are really talking more about a general tendency on the part of Hellenistic Judaism to transmit the Hebrew Old Testament and to compose certain religious texts than about a specific collection of documents whose text was established and whose limits were defined by some ecclesiastical authority.

One fact does seem to obtrude from the history of the translation of the Old Testament into Greek. Whereas Palestinian Judaism retained the reading of the Hebrew text in the synagogue service with its reading of the Aramaic Targum, the Greek version appears to have replaced the Hebrew text in practically all facets of Hellenistic Judaism. The situation in the Diaspora would thus be related to the situation in Palestine in somewhat the same way as modern Protestantism is related to Roman Catholicism. During the Latin Mass the Epistle and Gospel lections are read in Latin at their appropriate places in the Mass, but just before the sermon a translation of the Gospel into the vernacular is read, and frequently a translation of the Epistle as well. In Protestant and Reformed Churches, the Scripture lesson is read only in the vernacular; sometimes this is the Authorized Version, which is itself often in need of further " translating," and sometimes it is simply a more contemporary version that is used, such as the Revised Standard Version. The effect that these practices have had upon the religious vocabulary of Protestantism and Roman Catholicism serves as a background against which we may more adequately understand what happened in Hellenistic Judaism.

The Judaism of the Diaspora was markedly different from its parent and contemporary in Palestine. For many centuries the Hebrew religion had resisted being swallowed up by the Canaanite fertility cults, and it had also succeeded in excluding that tendency toward syncretism which might have made it a more successful missionary religion. For anyone to become a member of the Israelite community, it was necessary to renounce his ties with the culture in which he had been born and reared. Because Palestinian Judaism was, to all intents

and purposes, coextensive with the Jewish nation, the missionary problem was not really presented since there were few,
if any, candidates for initiation into the community. Once the
Jewish community began to spread along the trade routes of
the Middle East, however, the entire problem of apologetic
arose, and with it came the missionary problem. The crux of
the matter was represented in the fact that Greeks and other
non-Jewish peoples could hear the sacred scriptures of the
Jews read in the language which they spoke and understood.
Likewise, Jews who were many generations removed from
Palestine heard the scriptures read and expounded in the same
tongue as that in which they conversed and carried on business
transactions. While the Judaism of the Diaspora did not at
first consciously undertake a missionary effort, non-Jews who
spoke Greek were attracted by the virility and moral purity of
Judaism.

The terms in which some of these more sensitive non-Jews
might have expressed the moral purity of Judaism were those
involving promiscuous relations between the sexes. The negative attitude of Judaism with regard to such relations was not
born of any moralistic tendency, however, but arose out of the
peculiar history of Israel. Both the Pentateuch and the Prophets
bear testimony to the basic reason for the Jewish prohibition
of promiscuity. One of the characteristics of the fertility cult
against which prophets since the days of Elijah had waged
unceasing war was a mimetic rite in which temple prostitutes
participated in the hope that the Baal could be induced to
grant fertility to the land. With the passage of time and the
change in historical situation, the victory achieved by Yahwism
over Baalism was generalized into the principle that promiscuity is the equivalent of idolatry. Thus, the "moral purity"
of Judaism was, in reality, another expression of that strict
monotheism which is verbalized in the First Commandment
and in the daily prayer of the Jew known as the Shema (Deut.
6:4 f.). The virility of Judaism was also a product of its peculiar history, for in maintaining his religion the Jew also af-

firmed his patriotism. Judaism preserved its communal status because it was more than a voluntary religious community; the God of Israel, who was the Lord of Creation, had chosen this community for his own, and no matter how it might be scattered, it was still the *populus Dei.*

It would be a mistake to contend that Judaism of the Diaspora made many converts, for the lot of a person who submitted to circumcision was a share in the sufferings inflicted upon the Jews from time to time by a hostile Gentile populace. This Gentile populace could hardly regard the Jews as other than foreign interlopers who resisted assimilation and enjoyed certain exemptions from the observances required of full citizens. In some respects, the Jews were given the same status as nations now accord diplomatic personnel from another nation; the difference was, of course, that the Jews of the Diaspora were permanent residents of the Hellenistic cities. Nevertheless, there was a considerable group of non-Jews who were drawn to the ethical rather than the ceremonial aspects of the religion professed by this alien community. The interaction between the Jews of the Diaspora and these "God fearers" together with the response of the Jews to their hostile neighbors created an atmosphere which was decidedly different from that in which Palestinian Judaism lived and practiced its religion.

As Hellenistic Jews sought to defend themselves and their religion against intellectual derogation, they developed an apologetic literature that was distinctive. They were at a considerably greater advantage over their brethren in Palestine because they already possessed a sacred scripture written in the language spoken by their opponents. In part at least, these Jewish apologists shared the viewpoint of those whom they addressed. The common language assisted greatly in communication. By far the most important center from which this sort of writing emanated was Alexandria in Egypt. Although Alexandrian Jews produced many types of literature much of which is no longer extant, it seems quite clear that whatever these Jews wrote was intended to answer criticism and demonstrate the superiority of Judaism over its many pagan rivals. Of the two best-known apologists for Hellenistic Judaism, Philo (d. ca. A.D. 50) was an Alexandrian and Josephus (A.D. 37–ca.100) was a Palestinian who became Hellenized. Philo's voluminous works were all written and composed in the Greek of one who had grown up in the Hellenistic world, but Josephus tells us in the preface of his first work, *On the Jewish War*, that he composed it originally in Aramaic and then translated it into Greek. Josephus was primarily a historian, as indicated by both his major works: *On the Jewish War*, in seven books, and *The Antiquities of the Jews*, in twenty books. On the other hand, Philo was distinctly a philosopher, although his medium of expression was chiefly a running commentary on the Pentateuch or monographs dealing with specific subjects arising out of the Pentateuch.

No doubt the most important contribution to the interchange between Hellenistic culture and Judaism was made by Philo. Unlike most other Hellenistic Jews, he was a philosopher and went to the core not only of Hellenistic thinking but of Jewish thinking as well. While there are traces of allegory in Jewish literature before Philo, he is the first to employ this method of interpretation in a systematic way. The Wisdom of Solomon and the Letter of Aristeas both employed allegory as a hermeneutic principle, but their use of this tool of interpretation is only occasional and incidental. (Cf. Wisd. of Sol. 10:7, using Gen. 19:26; 10:17, using Ex. 13:21; 16:6 f., using Num. 21:9; 18:24, using Ex. 28:4. Letter of Aristeas 147, using Lev. 11:13-21; 150, using Lev. 11:3; 153, using Lev. 11:4.) By means of consistent and systematic use of allegory, Philo developed to its acme the idea that whatever was noble in Greek thinking was to be discovered in the sacred scripture of Judaism. He had had for predecessors in this enterprise, in addition to those just mentioned, a lost work called *An Explanation of the Mosaic Law* attributed to one Aristobolus, and that work which most nearly approaches his style, IV Maccabees, written just shortly before the active period of Philo's writing career. In Philo, the communication between alien Judaism and indigenous Hellenistic culture achieved its highest point. His thirty-eight extant works mark him out as at once a prolific and diversified author. Nevertheless, Philo's fame is due to the Christian church, which adopted him, rather than to his own people, who soon rejected his approach to the problem of communication.

For whatever causes, the Jews abandoned the effort to cross the gap between themselves and the Hellenistic world. The task was taken up by their successor, the Christian church. There are several historical reasons for the change in the attitude of the Jews toward bridging the chasm that separated them from the Hellenistic world. The rise of the Gentile mission undertaken by the Christians coincides roughly with the last decade or so of Philo's life; at approximately the time of Philo's death, the distinguished career of the apostle Paul was entering its most decisive phase. Meanwhile, the center of political hegemony had shifted to Rome now ruled by the famous general Vespasian, who was the military architect of the siege and destruction of Jerusalem less than two decades after Philo's death. The success of the Christian mission to Gentiles begun in the Syrian city of Antioch meant that the Christian church became much more Gentile than Jewish in the last quarter of the first century.

In order to preserve the weapons in its religious arsenal from capture by the Christian church and ultimate use against them, the Jews were forced to regroup and emphasize their peculiarity rather than continue the apologetic mission to Hellenism. The Christian church began to move into the Hellenistic world in force, in the meantime, and to make good use of the lines of communication established by the Hellenistic synagogues. Meanwhile, toward the end of the first century, the Jews began to concentrate their energies upon the homeland. One phase of the campaign on the home front was an attempt to recoup the political losses suffered in the war with the Romans (A.D.

66–70); this phase of the campaign met with total failure when the last vestiges of Jewish hegemony were finally eradicated by the Romans during the principate of Hadrian (A.D. 135) and the Holy City was completely Romanized even to its new name, Aelia Capitolina.

Another aspect of the campaign undertaken by Judaism to reassert its separateness and peculiarity was much more successful. Not all the Jews who departed from Palestine moved westward. The earliest dispersions of the Jews were the result of conquests from the East. In the late eighth century B.C., the Assyrians overcame the Northern Kingdom of Israel; the territory was reorganized into Assyrian provinces, many Israelites were deported to the East, and immigrants from Mesopotamia were settled in their place. Although the Southern Kingdom of Judah successfully resisted invasion and annexation by Assyria, this final remnant of the glorious kingdom once ruled by David and Solomon met a similar fate at the hands of the Babylonian invader in a series of events which culminated in 586 B.C. As in the case of the Northern Kingdom, so it was with Judah; in fact, the deportation of Judahites came to be known as *the* exile. Even if the numbers of those deported to Babylon were not so great as the Biblical narrative would lead us to believe, the deportees included a great number of those who could be called the religious leaders of Judah.

From the Babylonian exile onward, there was a significant, if not excessively large, community of Jews who resided in Babylon. This community in dispersion never essayed a missionary effort among the Babylonians, despite the fact that it would conceivably have been easier here than among the Greeks because of the close affinity between the tongues spoken by the Jews and the Babylonians. Perhaps this very close affinity of language between captives and captors, together with the bitter hatred engendered by the long and cruel war between Judah and the Babylonians, forced the Jews in Babylon jealously to guard their uniqueness. In any event, it was this Babylonian community which provided the impetus and the means by which the Palestinian Jews began their withdrawal from the Hellenistic mission in the late first and early second centuries of our era. The closing of the canon of Hebrew scriptures toward the end of the first century, the suppression of noncanonical literature such as the Hebrew original of the book of Ecclesiasticus, and the fixing of the text of the Hebrew Old Testament by the Masoretes were but manifestations of the general xenophobia of the brand of Judaism that gained and kept the upper hand from the late first century A.D. onward. Exclusivity dominated this religious community from that point; the Judaism we know from the second century until modern times is the direct descendant of this movement.

Where the Jews had left off their missionary thrust into the Greco-Roman world the Christians took it up. Equipped with a religious vocabulary and a sacred scripture in the lingua franca of the sprawling Mediterranean dominions that had passed from Macedonian control to Roman rule, the Christian church was able to capitalize on its patrimony and press the advantage enjoyed by Judaism. One of the most striking features of the Christian missionary effort from the end of the first century is the almost complete absence of an active Judaism that spoke Greek. Whatever Jewish polemic was made against the Christian claims, it was written in Mishnic Hebrew or Aramaic by and for Jews. Thus the Bible of the Christian church which missionized the Greco-Roman world was a ready-made document in the language of those to whom the mission was addressed. The New Testament, which was composed in this Hellenistic environment, was based upon the Greek version of the Old Testament, while Christian missionary and apologetic literature employed both the vocabulary and the thought structure of Hellenistic Judaism, chiefly that of Alexandria.

B. Ante-Nicene Christianity

The story of the struggle engaged in by Christians to expand the vocabulary of Hellenistic Judaism must be seen in conjunction with the parallel struggle to protect the older and newer levels of the Christian vocabulary from misunderstanding by the Greeks who became Christians as well as by those who did not actually enter the community of the church. The history of Christian thought can be traced along a series of points at which misunderstanding arose. The vast Gnostic movement, which plagued the church in the second century, is the prime instance of a movement that seized and exploited the vocabulary of the church and turned it inside out. Taking its point of departure inside the young and growing church, this movement consisted of various sects and groups that professed to have greater knowledge (gnōsis) about those very matters which comprised the core of Christian belief and practice. Gnostics and Christians alike could be said to stem from the Hellenistic Judaism that achieved its zenith in Philo. It was no accident that Pantaenus, Clement, and Origen accomplished their work in Alexandria, where Philo had made his mark and prominent Gnostics probably taught and wrote in the second century. These early great defenders of orthodoxy recaptured the vocabulary, and with boldness and imagination they turned the method employed by the Gnostics into a weapon against them.

Once the church was recognized by the state at the beginning of the fourth century, new problems arose concerning the vocabulary in which the Christian faith was proclaimed and discussed. One of the most successful moves for commending the church to the Hellenistic world was taken by such early apologists as Quadratus, Aristides, Justin, Melito, and Athenagoras when they adopted the philosophical approach. They could expound the Christian faith systematically in terms of the Platonic system, which had undergone several revisions since the classical period and had become the philosophical framework in which religious inquiry was prosecuted. While this bold stroke by the apologists advanced the Christian cause in the second and third centuries, it produced a backlash in the fourth and fifth centuries. The problem faced by the Council of Nicaea in 325 was engendered by a too rigid adherence

to those very Platonic categories which had proved so useful
in the hands of the apologists. The Arian controversy, which
led to the convening of the Council of Nicaea, was basically
an argument over the meaning of terms applied to Jesus as the
Son of God. Although it was met and dealt with at Nicaea, the
controversy exercised the church for most of the fourth century; the last of Arianism was not heard, however, until the
end of the fifth century (A.D. 496) when the Frankish tribes
were converted to Roman Catholicism.

Arianism derived its name from an Alexandrian presbyter
named Arius (ca. 250–ca. 336). This Neoplatonist tried by
means of classical philosophy to resolve a problem that had occupied the church ever since the second century and could
even be traced back into the New Testament. Several formu-
las had been proposed whereby the unique filial reationship of
Jesus to God the Father could be expressed. In response to the
two opposite positions, one maintaining that Jesus was "mere
man" (adoptionism) and the other contending that the three
so-called "persons" of the Trinity were only different modes
of divine activity (Sabellianism), Arius proposed a solution
that made of Christ a typical intermediary being of Neoplatonic theology. While his proposal protected the independence
of Christ's being against the Sabellians, it fell under the same
condemnation as that leveled against the adoptionists, since it
subordinated Christ's being and denied the finality of God's
action in Christ. The issue thus proposed by Arius was whether
or not the classical and pagan thought was to survive as the
ultimate categories in which the Christian revelation was to be
expressed. The Council of Nicaea countered Arius with the
declaration of a symbol or creed which embodied the funda-
mentals in the affirmation of New Testament Christianity, the
ultimate basis being found in the text: "The Logos became
flesh and dwelt in our midst" (John 1:14; my own translation).

The conciliar solution to this problem amounted to an entirely different approach to this vexing problem of how the
Son is related to the Father. Classical thought had always pro-

ceeded *from nature to God;* thus the basic category was nature. The Nicene Fathers, reiterating what had been maintained in both literature and tradition prior to Nicaea, proceeded *from God to nature;* the basic category here was history.[1] Such a reorientation of approach to the fundamental problems of being and existence could not help creating utter chaos in theological discussion between the "orthodox" and the "heretics." The declaration of the church shattered the framework in which discussion could take place; terms used by orthodox Christianity did not have the same meaning as they had for centuries in Neoplatonic circles. The reasons for this impasse are to be sought in the dual origin of the Christian proclamation. In order to appreciate some of the dimensions of this dual origin and the difficulties it engendered, a retrospective glance is in order.

Jesus and his disciples spoke Aramaic, a language closely related to the Hebrew in which the greater portion of the Old Testament was written, and akin to the Arabic spoken throughout the Middle East today. From all that we can ascertain about the apostolic band to whom the church owes its origins, it is very unlikely that any of them were at all fluent in any other tongue. Simple fishermen like Simon, whose other name was Cephas (Aramaic for " rock ") or Peter (the Greek equivalent for " Cephas "), or the brothers Zebedee, John and James, to whom was given the name Boanerges (the derivation of which is quite uncertain although it is probably of Semitic origin; cf. Mark 3:17), would have had little, if any, occasion to know any language except Aramaic. It is more than probable that all these men, Jesus included, knew practically no Hebrew, for by their time Hebrew had become a classical tongue. What they knew of the Old Testament they learned from the regular synagogue translation into Aramaic known as a Targum. Indeed, some parts of the Old Testament had actually been composed in Aramaic; portions of The Book of Daniel (Dan. 2:4 to 7:28) and of The Book of Ezra are known to us only in this west Semitic tongue that had been spoken for a long time in

Northern Syria and Mesopotamia and ultimately became the traffic language of the Babylonian Empire and its successor, the Persian Empire.

We are dependent for our knowledge of what Jesus preached and the meager details of his life, however, upon completely Greek sources. There are no Aramaic remnants of the Gospels or those documents which preceded them. The entire New Testament is a collection of documents that are Greek through and through. Certain parts of the Gospels, notably the small collections of Jesus' sayings in Mark and the somewhat longer catenae of these sayings in Matthew and Luke, bear the marks of Aramaic language and style although in translation; the same may be said of certain large sections of the first fifteen chapters of the book of The Acts and of considerable portions of the book of Revelation. Nevertheless, the New Testament, including even those portions in which the Aramaic flavor is somewhat pronounced, was written by and for men to whom Greek was not only a familiar language but was actually their native language. The letters of Paul, the tract attributed to the chief of the apostles and known as I Peter, the homily attributed to James, and the elaborate composition of the unknown author to the Hebrews are all outstanding samples of rhetorical Greek of the first century A.D.

For whatever reasons may be adduced to account for the drastic change in the linguistic medium of communication employed by Christians during the first few decades of their history, the fact of the change is most significant. To have changed to another language within the Semitic group would have been drastic enough, but to have crossed the gulf between the Semitic and Indo-European language groups produced many problems. These were to increase geometrically as the church sought both to articulate its faith for its own constituency and to defend that articulation of the faith against misunderstanding outside the community as well as within. There were in this process two different types of problems; one of them centered upon the teaching of Jesus himself and the other upon the church's teaching concerning the person and work of Jesus.

So far as it is possible by critical means to sift out of the Gospels what Jesus actually preached and the reasons for his having been condemned to a conspirator's death, all the evidence seems to point toward a state of affairs which could be understood only in terms of the religious milieu peculiar to the early first century in Palestine. The challenge posed by the preaching of Jesus is first and foremost a challenge to the constituted authority of the Jewish religious community. The basic stratum of the Christian tradition is therefore inevitably involved in the historical fortunes and destiny of a particular people the story of whose past is told in the Old Testament. The gist of the story is quite simple and straightforward. In a series of historical events involving the Israelite nation, Yahweh, the God of Israel who was understood to be creator and sustainer of the entire world, had chosen this nation and delivered it thereby revealing his nature. The choice or election of Israel demanded a response to Yahweh on Israel's part; the course of Israel's history as related in its sacred scriptures demonstrated how this nation had responded at times and defected from this response at others. The central thrust of the preaching of Jesus was set against this historical background and reiterated in pithy saying or more involved but no less pointed parable or story the continuing demand for a response from this nation which had been so singularly treated by Yahweh. The burden of the message was that the time was short, but that Yahweh could be trusted to carry out his promise to the responding community as well as to effect his judgment upon the community that failed to respond. Therefore, it is quite clear that the preaching of Jesus was rooted and grounded in history — the history of a particular people.

It is further clear from a critical reading of the Gospel narrative that Jesus was put to death by the Roman authority in Judea for conspiracy or what should probably be specified as fomenting revolution against lawful authority. The Roman

authority in Judea most likely worked in somewhat close conjunction with the Jewish political organization in the fashion
of any military government in an occupied territory. The Jewish local political authority, which was coextensive with the
religious authority, sensed the threat involved in Jesus' proclamation of the imminence of a decisive act by Yahweh. It moved
quickly to denounce Jesus to the Roman governor, the Procu-
rator Pontius Pilate, contending that Jesus was a dangerous
and subversive leader whose continued presence could threaten
both the good order of the occupied territory and the hegemony of the occupying power. The chances are more than quite
good that Pontius Pilate neither understood the specific nature
of the crime of which Jesus stood accused nor could have understood the tone and meaning of what Jesus actually preached.
What was probably decisive for him was that in the specifica-
tion the terminology of kingdom was employed, albeit Jesus
spoke of the Kingdom or Reign of God; further, the recognized
subordinate native authority had denounced him as a threat
to the Roman hegemony that Pilate was charged to protect
with the aid, if necessary, of the Roman legionary troops assigned to the legate of Syria. Exercising his proper authority,
Pilate ordered that Jesus be executed as a traitor along with a
couple of brigands who had been apprehended in treasonable
acts.

At this stage of its development, the history of Jesus and his
preaching could make sense only to a people that had been
accustomed to thinking in terms that are peculiar to the Israelite community. The challenge posed by Jesus was spoken with
a self-authenticating power that demanded a response. That response might be acceptance, or it might be rejection as in the
case of the scribes and Pharisees or the Sadducees who flatly
denied the authenticity of his message. The most important
thing to be noticed about this stratum of the history is that it
is comprehensible only in the Semitic milieu in which Israelite
religion and its development into Judaism were nurtured.
During this stage of its life, the proclamation was made in the

Semitic tongue of Aramaic and was couched in the terms of a particular framework of thinking which was indigenous to Judaism and due in no small measure to the properties of that language family in which Jewish thought was prosecuted.

After the death of Jesus, if not before, there was considerable reflection among those who responded to his message; this reflection centered upon the questions of who he was and what he had accomplished or was in the process of accomplishing. Some further events involving Jesus and the disciples became the New Testament vehicle for expressing the results of that reflection. Very soon after Jesus had been executed on the cross, that band of disciples who had been most intimately associated with him during his active ministry of preaching the nearness of God's Reign shared a number of experiences in which they became acutely aware that he was surely living again. At first, they were not at all sure *how* he had been delivered from death, but they were unshakably convinced *that* death no longer held him. They articulated this experience and the assurance that came from it in terms of a historical statement: God had raised him from the dead (cf. I Cor. 15:4). What specifically was involved in this assertion took some time and further experience to work out. The terms in which it was worked out were, again, peculiarly Jewish both in language and in thought form. Probably the earliest of the ways in which the community expressed this fundamental conviction involved an application to Jesus of the language in which he himself had spoken.

Throughout the four Gospels in the words attributed to Jesus there are a number of occurrences of the term " Son of Man." It is possible to separate and classify these occurrences of the term according to the affinity between this figure and Jesus himself. At the lowest level of affinity can be classified such utterances as Mark 8:38 and 13:26; in each of these instances, Jesus seems to be using the term to apply to a heavenly personage at whose coming " in clouds " the final judgment will take place and God will gather all his dispersed *populus* at the holy Mt. Zion, after which the Son of Man, as God's vice-gerent, will exercise the rule of God over that *populus*. In such passages as these, there appears to be a clear line of demarcation between Jesus and this Son of Man (cf. Dan., ch. 7); here, Jesus echoes a popular hope for a heavenly redeemer such as one might have heard among apocalyptic sects, such as the Qumrân community. At the extreme opposite of the scale can be classified those sayings attributed to Jesus in which the identity of Jesus with this heavenly figure is beyond any question or doubt (cf. Mark 8:31; 9:31; 10:33 f., 45, etc.). Since the designation "Son of Man" is primarily a term employed in Jewish eschatology, it is highly unlikely that this identification between Jesus and that heavenly figure could have taken place in any but the most Jewish milieu. The fact that the use of the term in the Gospels is limited to Jesus' own words, plus the fact that as a category for understanding the life and ministry of Jesus it figures in none of the other literature of the New Testament lead us to suspect that the term was one of the casualties in the linguistic change from Semitic to Indo-European.

A similar though not completely parallel occurrence is to be noted in the case of another term employed as a category for evaluating Jesus' effect, that of Messiah. Used very early to express the role played by Jesus, it made sense only in the purely Semitic Jewish context of Palestinian Judaism. A term of venerable ancestry in the history of Israel used to designate those anointed (*maschiach*) to carry out the work of Yahweh, it had been used of David (II Sam. 19:21; 22:51; 23:1; Ps. 18:50; 89:38, 51; 132:10, 17; cf. Ps. 2:2; 20:6; 28:8) as well as of Samuel and of Saul (I Sam. 12:3, 5; 24:6, 10; 26:9, 11, 16, 23); it had even been used of the Persian Cyrus (Isa. 45:1). In later Judaism, *maschiach* became the designation of the one whom Yahweh would raise up to deliver his people from foreign oppression and to rule as His surrogate in the day when the enemies of Yahweh, who were Israel's enemies, would be subjugated. The word was translated from its later Aramaic form and became *Christos* (from *chrizo*, "anoint," Greek).

Once it entered the Greek language, however, this term became a proper name applied to Jesus and was not translated again but remained in the Greek form as all of our modern language versions of the New Testament amply demonstrate. The peculiar significance of the term was lost, however, in this process of translation and application as a proper name; its eschatological meaning escapes notice when it is used as a proper name. Nevertheless, behind the proper name is a designation that ties Jesus inextricably to the history and eschatological hope of the Jewish community of the late first century.

In the few short years that intervened between the height of Jesus' ministry and the mission of Paul to the Hellenistic cities in which there were Greek-speaking Jewish synagogues, a decided change had taken place in the message as well as the structure of this small band of Jesus' followers. The message of Jesus to the elect people of God had become the message about what God had done in Jesus for the redemption of the entire created world (cf. II Cor. 5:18 f.). This change was but one step, albeit a decisive one, in the course of development of the Christian church. While Jesus and his disciples, together with the rest of that early band who had known him during his lifetime and become aware of him as living again, were completely Semitic in language and, more importantly, in outlook, the second generation of the church contemporary with Paul could be said to have a Jewish outlook *despite* their language limitation to Greek. The next generations of Christians were successively less Jewish in the outlook, however, and were Greek not only in language but in thought pattern as well. What protected them from becoming totally Hellenistic in viewpoint was their retention of the Greek Old Testament and the recognition of the literature produced by the early Greek-speaking Church as a normative and canonical scripture which they called the *New* Testament (covenant). The increasingly Greek Church was further prevented from complete Hellenization by a liturgical life which was rooted in the earliest generation of the church's existence and which rehearsed in ritual and

ceremonial the events constitutive of its existence. This covenant ceremonial served as a balance wheel in the community
because, no matter how the language of theological discussion
might react to the questions which were being asked and answered in open forum, the liturgy was the conservator of the
constitutive events even for those who did not or could not
read the documents that constituted the scripture.

Thus, while the Christian church was exploiting the missionary channels opened by Hellenistic Judaism to the Gentile
world, the very tools forged by Hellenistic Judaism protected
the church from complete severance of the ties which bound
it to that alien culture resident in the Gentile world. The
church stood astride the boundary between Hellenistic and
Semitic cultures, preserving its primary rootage in the historic past of a community that had all but ceased to exist.

C. Nicaea and Beyond

During the first three centuries of our era, the Christian
church successfully avoided two possible disastrous alternatives
and became the most potent force in Europe from the fall of
Rome until the rise of nationalism. On the one hand, there was
a strong tendency for the church to become so thoroughly
identified with the culture of Greece and ultimately of Rome
that it would have been swallowed up as but one more of the
many religious movements which were born in the Near Orient
only to wither away in the busy market places of the Mediterranean basin. By skillful reinterpretation of the basic affirmation given in terms of a particular series of historical events,
the Christian church escaped the fate of such cults as that of
Isis, Cybele, Syra Dea, and an incalculable number of others
which gave way before new ones spawned in the fertile area
bordering the eastern Mediterranean. Christianity's successful
resistance to the threats posed from within by Marcion, the
Gnostics, and so many others great and small is a testimony to
its ability to retain its uniqueness while continuing its aggres-
sive mission.

The clue to this success will be found, to a large measure, in its retention of the Old Testament and the liturgical structure of Judaism which constituted a hold upon its fundamentally Semitic outlook. Restriction of attendance upon the inner liturgy to those who had been baptized together with the more or less open character of the public liturgy was a manifestation of the bipolar life of the community. The inner liturgy of the Eucharist stemmed from the family type Seder, which was a representation in anamnesis of the exodus; the public liturgy was a continuation of the synagogue service, which centered on the reading of the sacred scriptures. When these two services were joined, the inner character of the latter portion of the liturgy was preserved by restricting those who could remain to those who were incorporated into the family — the community whose history was to be found in the life of the Israelite people.

On the other hand, there was an equally strong tendency for the church to withdraw completely from the intellectual and cultural conversation that took place among the plethora of religions abroad in the Mediterranean world. Judaism had abandoned the missionary enterprise, and except for that sectarian and separatist community which owed its origin to the rabbinic reorganization in the second century in Palestine and Babylon, it ceased to exist as a force in the religious life of the Hellenistic world. One of the deepest mysteries of ancient history is the story of the decline and ultimate disappearance of Hellenistic Judaism. Within the church this tendency was represented by the dour North African, Tertullian (ca. 160–ca. 220), who had performed singularly heroic service against the followers of Marcion. His departure from the frontier of the church's encounter with the Hellenistic world is all the more significant in the light of his stellar performance as a defender of the faith, but it is also partly to be explained from his stance as a defender. Enamored of the rigidity of Montanism, to which he was likely drawn by his own ascetic leanings, this church father eschewed the forum of conversations with non-Christians by his famous utterance: "What has Athens to do

with Jerusalem? What has the Academy to do with the church?
What have heretics to do with Christians?" [2] His following
was not small, but the central strain of the church's thought
and conversation followed the direction pointed by Clement of
Alexandria and Origen. This pathway was to prove more a
precarious trail than a broad highway, but it led to open con-
test with pagan thought rather than to fortified security inside
impregnable walls. The victory achieved by the Christian
church in its attempt to express the gospel in alien Hellenistic
forms was not gained without casualties, as the case of Origen
so eloquently demonstrates, and the victor emerged from the
fray with visible scars of battle.

The decisive intellectual battle was fought with Greek
thought in the course of the fourth century; the fifty years
between the adoption of the Nicene Creed and its ratification
at Constantinople decided the issue although it would be
another century before the Christian church would have a
philosophy. The terms in which the issue was joined were
themselves a product of the transfer from the Semitic idiom
to the Greek. On Semitic grounds the gospel proclaimed a decisive act of God in which Jesus played a unique role; as the
anointed and elect messenger of God he announced this decisive act and was instrumental in bringing it to pass. This is the
very point of the designation of Jesus as Messiah-Christ or as
Son of Man. On Hellenistic grounds, however, the issue turned
upon the relationship that existed between Jesus and God;
here, the emphasis lay upon Jesus' role as Son of God and
Logos. The question was posed in peculiarly Greek terms, and
the historical categories of eschatology were overshadowed by
the logical categories of classical philosophy. Thus, the theological problem which vexed the fourth-century church involved the religious and theological language of paganism and
demanded whether or not the language was adequate to carry
the uniqueness of the gospel proclamation.

The problem over which the battle was fought in the fourth
century was born within the Christian community of the

second generation, which was still rather amphibious by virtue of the Semitic overtones that echoed behind its Greek language. The easiest point at which to see the problem is in the Prologue to the Fourth Gospel (John 1:1-18). In the Greek it is sufficiently ambiguous so that a Christian of Jewish background could have read it with one meaning, but a Christian of pagan Hellenistic background could have read it and gained from it a significantly different meaning. The crux of the matter is in the Greek word *logos* that is translated in the Authorized Version, and in every official English version since, by the English term "Word" (John 1:1, 14). To the Christian of Jewish background the Greek word *logos* recalls immediately how God created the world by his "word" (Ps. 33:6, 9; Wisd. of Sol. 9:1; cf. Gen. 1:1 to 2:4). To such a reader, in fact, the entire Prologue of the Fourth Gospel would read like a commentary on the first chapter of Genesis. In the translation of ideas, however, the term *logos* both adds and subtracts with reference to the Hebrew term that lies behind it. A convert to the Christian church whose previous education and upbringing had been in the theological and philosophical milieu created by Neoplatonism would, on the contrary, hear echoes of Logos theology. For him it would call to mind a whole train of thought which goes back to the fifth-century B.C. Greek philosopher Heraclitus. The Stoics popularized the notion of Logos as universal reason, and in Neoplatonism the Logos was conceived as the highest in a series of intermediary agents between God and the world. It is no wonder, then, that a Christian of Greek education and Greek mind would hear something different behind the Prologue of the Fourth Gospel; it would sound to him like a paean of praise extolling the divine Reason which is but little lower than God.

The etymology of the two words, one in Greek and the other in Hebrew, illuminates the conflict which is behind the translation. Both come from verbs which were used to signify the act of speaking, but each has its own peculiar history. Behind the Hebrew verb *dabar* is the notion of leading something

forth; hence, it is a dynamic concept and issues in the secondary meaning of " deed, act." On the other hand, the Greek verb
arises from a notion of gathering or grasping; *legō* originally
means " to collect," and it is used to mean " speak, say " as but
one of its many uses all of which have to do with intellectual
activity. The secondary meaning of the noun *logos* that is derived from the verb is "reason"; hence, it is a more or less
static notion intimately associated with intellectually grasping
reality. Although the distinction was lost in translation, it sur-
vived in the Jewish milieu, Hellenistic or Palestinian, by virtue
of a total impress made by the Biblical outlook; as the church
became more Greek, however, it could not help being lost almost beyond recovery.

The Arian controversy centered upon the basic meaning of
words, a struggle to define in communicable terms the basic
proclamation of the gospel. In order to clear up the problem,
it was necessary to stipulate the way in which certain key
words were to be used and understood. The terms on which
the controversy hinged were *logos* and " Son," both of which
occur in juxtaposition in the opening chapter of the Fourth
Gospel.[3] Arius and his followers chose a path previously
marked out by Ignatius of Antioch (ca. 35–ca. 107) and more
carefully delineated by the apologists of the second and early
third centuries. While the Arians went to Greek philosophy
for the meaning of *logos*, the more temperate non-Arians,
taught by Irenaeus of Lyons (ca. 130–ca. 200), leaned more
decidedly in the direction of the Bible and its Semitic idiom of
thought and expression. The Council of Nicaea set forth a
symbol to which it demanded subscription by all those who
should henceforth be esteemed orthodox, but the Council did
not set forth a specific interpretation of that creed to which
subscription was required. The exposition of that creed into
a philosophical framework remained the task of Athanasius of
Alexandria (ca. 296–373) in the East and Augustine of Hippo
(354–430) in the West. The problem was far from solved, however, for the way was left open for further speculation as to the

meaning of certain key terms used in the Niceno-Constantinopolitan Symbol. The pattern established at Nicaea was continued at each of the successive ecumenical councils. The church encouraged speculative thought and inquiry into the meaning of the creedal affirmations; in fact, the attitude of the church promoted the reinterpretation of words and statements in the context of pagan thought. Instead of laying down an elaborate explication of these symbols, however, the church tacitly reserved to itself a final judgment upon which of the expositions made by apologists and systematists were inimical to the foundation of the church's proclamation. Thus, in the course of the conversation with pagan thought, the church defended its proclamation in negative rather than in positive terms; that is to say, translation was encouraged, but the church exercised only a restraint upon the final validity of the translation. Each of the councils which were convened from the fourth through the seventh centuries dealt with a specific attempt to make a *systematic* explication of some vital aspect of the Christian affirmation. In each case, the council marked the line of development there discussed as a cul-de-sac or dead-end street.

The condemnation of Arius at Nicaea did not automatically put an end to Arianism, for the controversy seethed below the surface for five or six decades following Nicaea and frequently erupted in bitter conflict. The adoption of the Nicene Symbol struck the direction, however, and by means of its language, this creed protected the unity of God in diversity of activity. The problem which grew from this declaration was to occupy the church for a century and a half actively, and for more than three centuries off and on. From the time of Nicaea, the church began in earnest to attempt to express the uniqueness of Christ while protecting both his full participation in Godhead and his complete humanity.

When the church made its declaration on this issue at Chalcedon (451), it was the result of honest, if often overzealous, attempts to employ the structure of Neoplationism to express

a dynamic historical experience. Apollinarius of Laodicea (ca.
310–ca. 390) seized upon the threefold division of man that
had come down from Platonism; as a personal unity, he rea-
soned, man is a combination of body, animal, or irrational
soul, and rational, controlling, and directing soul. His solution
of the problem of how Christ could be a personal unity of
divinity and humanity was to envisage the replacement of the
human rational soul in the case of Christ by the divine Logos;
thus, the distinguishing feature of Christ was different from
that of ordinary men, but at the same time, Christ participated
in the ordinary world by way of animal soul and body. To
him, this was the most nearly perfect explication of the event
of Christ in the terms to which he was accustomed — those
of Greek philosophy. His Christological construction was condemned at Constantinople in 381. However, the *terms* in which
he posed the question were those in which the church argued
the question for three centuries, at least, until the rejection at
Constantinople in 681 of Monothelitism.

What is of particular value to our inquiry is the fact that
the church felt it necessary to speak *in terms of* classical philosophy as well as to speak *to* classical philosophy. In the conversation between pagan thought and the Christian church,
the terms of the pagan world were adopted, but they were
also adapted. Terms like " person," " nature," " substance,"
and " hypostasis " were not primarily Biblical and Hebraic
terms; they belonged to the world of classical philosophy. So
long as there existed a universal church, or the semblance of
one, an ecumenical council could be called to render a judgment on an effort at translation; this meant that the church
was serious about its communication, but it also meant that it
was serious about communicating what really was the gospel.
In this dialogue, the church gained its vocabulary which assured that it would be able to speak to the world and with the
world as long as that vocabulary had some meaning for the
world.

The lesson that we learn from even so brief and sketchy a

survey as the one we have attempted here is simply that communication even on the purely verbal level requires two participants. The main purpose served by this oversimplified outline is to set in its larger persepective the entire problem of language and Christian communication. We cannot possibly approach the multiphasic problem that confronts Christians in the twentieth century, even in its linguistic dimension, unless we can appreciate something of the undertaking in which the church has been engaged for twenty centuries. We are now called upon to speak to other Christians, some convinced and some only partly so, and to vast segments of the world that are non-Christian, anti-Christian, or pseudo-Christian; in this regard we are like our brethren whose history stretches centuries behind us. Even if we were able to understand that history in all its manifold nuances, a much more imperative task is to appreciate the tremendous pressures under which the church has lived and how these pressures have been responsible for the stance taken by the church in various crisis situations. Linguistically, we can see how the church's vocabulary has been forged in crisis and usually taken from the crisis itself.

We shall be delivered from one form or another of literalism if we can but appreciate that the language in which the church has spoken when it has been forced to make a declaration has been almost without exception determined by the threat that was being confronted. This principle applies as much to the New Testament as it does to any of the creedal statements to which the councils demanded subscription. In the final analysis, the Christian church is committed not to words or statements, no matter how sound or hallowed, but to the God who reveals himself redemptively in the act of Jesus the Christ and who continues his creative-redemptive work in and through that community the church wherein his Holy Spirit is active and effective. In order, however, that this allegiance may be made known, shared, and protected against misconstructions, it must be spoken about and discussed in language that is painfully inadequate. The only alternative to careful use of the language that is the current language is an abdication from the world which it is God's purpose to redeem and save from itself through the church.

Our own age is becoming acutely aware of the instrumentalism of language, but it is also keenly attuned to the fact that we must speak. Despite its transient quality, we must come to terms with language, the language in which we think and speak. If the historical dimension of the Christian dialogue with the world has taught us anything, it should have taught us that our primary task here is to listen to what philosophy is saying about language and through language. To what sort of linguistic milieu are we to address the Christian message? What in it will permit us to make that message meaningful in an age that is at least as inquisitive if not as inquiring as that during which the classical Christian vocabulary was formed?

Chapter II

Language and Religious Language:
The Philosophical Climate

A religious affirmation resembles more a poetic expression or a philosophical generalization than it does a simple empirical observation or a newspaper account of yesterday's baseball game. The language in which each of these statements is cast must be treated somewhat differently despite the fact that all may use the same general vocabulary and follow what are apparently the same basic rules of syntax. Because of the pioneering work undertaken by a group of mathematicians and scientists known as the Vienna Circle, we are now much more aware of the problems presented by statements that look similar but, in reality, are quite different. It would be quite erroneous, however, to limit recognition of the difficulties involved in dealing with different sorts of statements to modern times and to the logisticizing philosophers who have followed in the train of the Vienna Circle. As early as the eleventh century of our era, there was a continuing discussion over the precise value of what are known in Scholastic philosophy as universals. The terms in which linguistic analysis has been prosecuted in recent decades are a product of the world of natural science, logic, and mathematics. The medieval controversy over the value and meaning of universals was born in the realm of philosophical discourse and was carried on almost exclusively within the disciplines of philosophy and theology.

A. Nominalism Versus Realism

For the first several centuries of its existence in the Western world, the Christian church employed for its theological exposition the categories of Platonism. Because the Hellenistic world carried on its own theological discussion in a modified form of Platonism — Neoplatonism — the church found it both necessary and advantageous to expound its faith by way of this philosophical system. As we have already seen, most, if not all, of the acute problems of the conciliar period resulted from the use and misuse of the categories of Neoplatonism; it has also been evident that, despite these abuses, the church defined its faith in terms of this version of Platonism.

The philosophical system of the other great figure of ancient Greece, Aristotle, was generally regarded with suspicion among pagan as well as Christian theologians on the ground that it led to a materialistic view of the universe. Through the efforts of Porphyry (ca. 232–303), himself a Neoplatonist and an ardent anti-Christian, one important work of Aristotle did make its way into medieval thought. Porphyry wrote an extended introduction to the *Categories* of Aristotle, a portion of the larger *Organon;* the title of this work was *Isagoge,* which is Greek for "introduction." This work was translated from Greek into Latin by Victorinus Afer, the fourth-century Roman rhetorician and Neoplatonist theologian. A commentary upon this translation was made by Boethius (ca. 480–ca. 524), the Roman statesman-philosopher whose Neoplatonist works achieved popularity in Christian circles during the medieval period.

In the early medieval period, when the great bulk of Aristotle's work was practically unknown in Greek and hardly known at all even in Latin translation, Porphyry's *Isagoge* in the translation of Victorinus Afer, together with the commentary, served as a sort of textbook in the rudiments of logic. In the introduction to this work, Porphyry discussed such logical distinctions as genus and species, differentia, and char-

acteristic and accidental properties. Herein lay the seeds of
the controversy on universals which was to exercise theologians
of the eleventh through the thirteenth centuries.

During the early Middle Ages, most theologians would have
answered the question about the existence of universals, i.e.,
abstract concepts, in an essentially Platonic way by asserting
the existence of these concepts apart from the particulars in
which they were embodied. Thus, they would have been
giving testimony for their acceptance of the eternal world of
Ideas which was so characteristic of the Platonic scheme.
When Roscellinus (d. ca. 1125) proposed that these abstract
concepts were but exhalations of breath, he perpetrated a controversy that was brought to an end only by transition from
Platonism to Aristotelianism. The name given to his viewpoint,
nominalism, is actually derived from a later stage of the conflict, but it derives from the Latin word for "name," *nomen.*
Roscellinus was attacked vigorously by William of Champeaux
(ca. 1070–1121), who asserted in exaggerated form that these
concepts were *res* (things), and thus was begun the nominalist-realist battle over language and its meaning.

The middle ground between the two extremes was what
came to be known as conceptualism. This view owes its origin
really to Abélard (1079–1142), whose fame is broader than
his philosophical viewpoint alone might have won, and it was
ultimately brought to its fullest expression in Thomas Aquinas
(1225–1274). While the controversy seems to have little significance to us as we look at it in retrospect, it illuminates the
way in which the medieval church had begun to modify its
Platonic orientation in the direction of Aristotelianism. As
the church experimented with Aristotelianism, all the problems
that had apparently been settled during the conciliar period
were threatening to present themselves all over again.

As one side of the controversy developed, it became clear
that radical realism would lead inevitably to Sabellianism,
that heresy in which the three persons of the Trinity were but
unessential modifications of the essentially unitarian godhead.

On the other hand, radical nominalism would lead just as inevitably to the equally unacceptable view that the three persons of the Trinity were really separate gods; this tritheism would have upset the solution which came out of the Arian controversy and thus would have opened again a question that had been closed for some eight centuries.

The modified realism — or modified nominalism, depending on one's viewpoint — which can be traced from Abélard to Thomas denied the separate existence of universals but maintained the view that they really existed *in* things (*universale in re*). This view coincides approximately with that of Aristotle; it was on this point that Aristotle believed that he was in basic conflict with Plato. In essence, then, the Thomistic resolution of this problem amounted to a victory of Aristotle over Plato as the philosopher whose system was to be employed in expounding Christian doctrine. In effect, Thomas steered between nominalism and realism as the early church had steered between unitarianism and tritheism. Thus the transition was made from Platonism to Aristotelianism with a minimum of loss to the effort of the church to maintain contact with a changing philosophical scene. The ultimate acceptance of the Thomistic synthesis accounts for the Aristotelian context in which so many of the Reformation debates were carried on; it also explains, in part, the Aristotelian character of so much of the official Roman Catholic theology in modern times.

B. The Philosophy of Linguistic Analysis

The current trend in philosophy known variously as linguistic analysis, logical analysis, or logical empiricism is the result of a process similar to that which produced the nominalist-realist controversy and its eventual, if not ultimate, solution. One of the most important distinctions between Plato and Aristotle was the point of departure taken by each in the construction of his system. Plato began in mathematics, specifically geometry, and built a conceptual system that depended upon ideal forms; Aristotle, on the other hand, started from biology, and his systematic structure reflected his more empirical approach to reality. Something of the same distinction could be made between idealism and empiricism, although this will immediately be recognized as an oversimplification for purposes of discussion. At the end of the nineteenth century when the dominant philosophy was a type of idealism stemming from Hegel (1770–1831), a countermovement began which demanded greater clarity of expression. To such men as G. E. Moore and Bertrand Russell, the neo-idealists seemed to be talking about such exalted matters as "ultimate reality" in a language whose obscurity appeared to be an index of the profundity of the utterance. The upshot of this incipient revolution was the formation of the Vienna Circle, which included such figures as Rudolf Carnap and Maritz Schlick each of whom was in one way or another determined to bring philosophy into closer contact with the growing body of knowledge arising out of scientific inquiry. To this group of men and the students they attracted during the thirties of this century, all philosophy worthy of the name was a critique of language, and its chief aim was to show that all genuine knowledge about nature could be given expression in a language that was common to all the sciences.

When the leading proponents of linguistic analysis were forced to flee Europe, many of them found the United States hospitable to them. Here they began to publish again, under a new name, the successor to the journal previously published in Germany (*Erkenntnis*, Leipzig, 1931–1940); this journal became the *Journal of Unified Science*. With the help of interested Americans, they also undertook the compilation of the *International Encyclopedia of Unified Science*.[4] The influence of this school on philosophy in the United States was profound. Out of it grew what has been called logical positivism but which is more accurately designated "logical empiricism." In England, the influence is even greater since Ludwig Wittgenstein, from whom the Vienna Circle gained so much inspiration, was a lecturer at Cambridge before and after World War I and continued in this capacity until 1947. From the books and monographs that were published in these two countries during the early days of the movement, it became increasingly evident that this school of philosophy took its point of departure in the natural sciences and admitted no propositions that could not be verified in terms of sense experience.

The importance of the rise of this philosophical viewpoint — in the English-speaking world it is a vital contender for predominance — for the discussion between theology and philosophy becomes immediately apparent. At the outset, this school rules out as meaningless practically all the questions with which Christian theology has been actively concerned since its first appearance as a movement within Hellenistic Judaism. The only sorts of propositions which these linguistic analysts will admit are empirical statements — those which can be verified in terms of sense experience — and analytic statements which are of the logical or mathematical variety. With regard to the former, it is not necessarily indicated that they *must* be verified, but they must be *verifiable;* with regard to the latter, such a statement is considered a tautology, that is to say, it is true by definition. To this school of thought, logic and mathematics are actually only an intricate fabric of tautologies which provide the ground rules for the method whereby empirical statements are related to one another in the operation of thinking. All other statements, such as imperatives, attitude-statements, value judgments, and metaphysical statements (religious or otherwise), were at first consigned to a bin labeled " meaningless."

As this movement has gained ground, however, it has evinced a surprisingly mature concern for the kinds of statements which were originally ruled as inadmissible. Analytical and empirical statements require little attention once it is recognized that they are the sort of thing with which science and scientific observation is concerned; consequently, linguistic analysts are devoting a good deal of attention now to the method of treating poetic and artistic forms of expression as well as those types of statements which had formerly been excluded from consideration. While agreement is far from general among linguistic analysts, there does seem to be afoot a movement to extend the applicability of the *principle of verification* to certain types of statement previously exempted from this principle. At the same time efforts are being directed toward frank recognition that this principle is quite irrelevant to certain other types of statement.

In the case, for instance, of value statements, the role played by *criteria* of value is being explored with increasingly advantageous results for religious as well as nonreligious language. In the class of value statements, linguistic analysis includes not only such easily recognized value judgments as " this is a good saw " but also the kind of statement which makes a *moral* judgment. The procedure of verifying this sort of statement depends upon the delineation of the criteria that are employed in making the judgment. In many cases it will be readily apparent that disagreement about moral and value judgments arises from a disagreement about criteria. The only basis for overcoming an impasse between men and societies who count essentially different attitudes or actions as good is to refer the criteria to some sort of test to determine which set of criteria is the better. Because the judgment which would be rendered between two sets of criteria is itself a value judgment, it might appear that we have only compounded the problem. At this point, however, we are no longer discussing the value judgment itself but the method by which a value statement is to be verified. Unless there can be adduced a higher set of criteria according to which those involved in the original value statements can be judged — a set of criteria in which two representative speakers can share — there will be no resolution of the impasse. In other words, the value statement is verifiable only within very limited scope, and only when the criteria are mutually accepted.

While this sort of analysis does a great service by exposing the inadequacy of criteria involved in many more or less irresponsible value judgments, it also shows the utility of what we should have to call an absolute. The point of this observation can be clarified by juxtaposing two sentences which look alike but which belong to different classes according to linguistic analysis. "Sulphur is yellow" and "Hitler was evil" are two statements whose grammatical constructions are identical — each statement consists of a noun subject of which is predicated an adjectival modifier by means of the verb substantive. To determine the truth of either statement, or to verify it, it is necessary, however, to employ methods that differ radically. The color "yellow" is defined by certain agreed scientific principles, and to call the measurable wave lengths emitted by a pile of sulphur anything but yellow is simply gross misuse of words. That is to say, there is agreement about the meaning of "yellow," and even if a person is color-blind, he could be apprised of the truth of the statement by referring to an instrument for measuring the wave lengths of colors. It is not at all unusual, in fact, to define colors by their position on the spectrum produced by the refraction of white light through a prism.

On the other hand, the verification of the second statement depends upon the meaning of "evil"; here we cannot appeal to a universally accepted scale of numerical values nor even to a dictionary definition. What Hitler did or caused to be done can be judged in the same terms only by a community of speakers who share the same value criteria; two people from two different communities of speakers could agree on the factual description of what Hitler did or caused to be done, but the confirmed Nazi would judge these facts differently because he would be operating according to a different set of criteria from, let us say, those employed by a Jew whose parents died in a concentration camp. Unless the Nazi could be converted to the value criteria of the aforementioned Jew who made the judgment, or unless there could be introduced a scale of value criteria by which those employed by either of the speakers could be assessed, the statement could not be verified to the satisfaction of both speakers. Limited verification is in this case actually a barrier to the use of language as a viable means of communication between speakers.

Another sort of statement that received short shrift from the early proponents of linguistic analysis was the metaphysical statement. Into this class fall many, if not most, of those statements which concern theology and philosophy mutually. But many nonreligious statements dealing with "ideals" or "human rights" and other similar notions are also to be classified in this category. The current strain of linguistic analysis assigns to this class statements about which there is no general agreement either as to their meaning or as to the method by which they are to be verified. By this the linguistic analyst does not mean, as his predecessor in the thirties frequently did mean, that such statements are sheer nonsense or are simply unverifiable. What he does seem to mean is that there exists an identifiable class of statements which deal in ultimates and that such statements cannot be verified within the system to which they are ultimate. In this regard, they are much like value statements, for they depend upon criteria which in actual practice are not universally agreed upon.

In asking what an apparently metaphysical statement means, it is often possible to classify it with some other type of statement. For example, an apparently metaphysical statement such as "God is loving" may actually be an analytic statement. If we mean by "God" the one who is our loving Father, then such a statement is obviously a tautology in which subject and predicate are identical by definition. On the other hand, such a statement as "God was in Christ" (II Cor. 5:19) must remain in the class of metaphysical statements simply because the speaker means to convey information by it. An analytic statement actually conveys no information — that is, new information. But a metaphysical statement at least *purports* to convey information not otherwise ascertainable. The means by which a metaphysical statement is to be verified are not readily at hand because it would be implied that such means exist outside the system to which such statements are ultimate.

The contribution made to the clarification of thought by the philosophy of linguistic analysis is far from inconsiderable. It is a distinct advantage to realize that not all statements are alike even though they may agree in grammatical construction. A great deal of misunderstanding is to be avoided when it is admitted that different types of statements require different means of verification if they are to be established as true; the same applies to the recognition that not all means of verification are of a piece. The principle of verification is a useful tool for the clarification of thinking as well as of speaking. By their attention to those particular types of statements which present problems in regard either to meaning or verification or to both, the present proponents of linguistic analysis appear to be in process of modifying a prime tenet of the Vienna Circle, namely, that all metaphysical problems and all value problems are *merely* disguised language problems. Nevertheless, because philosophy has been so actively engaged in linguistic analysis for nearly thirty years, religious and theological thinkers have been prompted to face responsibly some of the problems involved in the language in which such thought has been prosecuted for so many centuries.

It may be convenient for certain types of theologians to dismiss the whole problem on the ground that metaphysical problems involve more than *mere* language problems, but responsible thought requires that even the small part of these problems assigned to the area of language be examined to test the hypothesis of linguistic analysis. One of the most important uses to which the principle of verification has been put is the rediscovery of what was really meant by the traditional arguments for the existence of God. Once it is admitted that no proof which could demand complete assent to the proposition "God exists" could ever be produced, we may not have advanced beyond Gaunilo or Kant, but a great deal of confusion is removed from religious and theological conversation merely by the reiteration of what Anselm's adversary so tellingly advanced.

It would be extremely encouraging to be able to report that the effect of theological thinking upon linguistic analysis has been as marked as the effect in the opposite direction; but there does not seem to be the slightest shred of evidence that (especially Christian) theological thinking has exerted any considerable influence upon modern linguistic analysis. The most that can be said in this regard — and it is not to be minimized — is that certain Christian philosophers and some fewer Christian theologians have been able to think effectively in this philosophic idiom. As representative of this intention to confront the Christian mind with the viewpoint championed by linguistic analysis, we should point out several recent writers.

John Wilson has written a deceptively brief study as an introduction to the problems that occupy the attention of linguistic analysts.[5] It would be difficult to recommend a more readable survey of the problems and the approach to them. As a survey, it is well suited for use as a primer for students who desire to get a firsthand view of this discipline. His more recent work is composed of a series of essays, some of which appeared in the *Hibbert Journal*. Each of them deals with a specific theological problem from the vantage point of linguistic analysis.[6] Both books have brief, but suggestive, bibliographies. Ian Ramsey, a professor at Oxford, explores the implications of linguistic analysis for a reformed Christian apologetic.[7] The content of this work is such that it may be used by teachers as a satisfactory second volume to follow Wilson's first, previously mentioned. Originally done as a series of lectures, Ramsey's book covers some of the material outlined by Wilson, but the alteration in perspective is helpful. Ben Kimpel's study of the semantic structure of religious language also grew out of a lecture series at Drew University.[8] Topically organized, it deals with problems similarly to Wilson's second volume. Indicative of the conversation produced by linguistic analysis at Oxford is a series of essays by several Oxonians edited by Basil Mitchell.[9]

C. The Philosophy of Symbolic Form

The effect of the radical development of linguistic analysis undertaken by the pupils of Wittgenstein, by Carnap and Charles Morris, and by Russell — to name but a few of the "greats" who are not all as intimately associated with the school as some — has been a new kind of positivism. Linguistic analysis produced logical analysis and a whole new epistemology that was the product of symbolic logicians such as Hans Reichenbach. Of Reichenbach, it has recently been said, "Every interpretation of life other than the physicochemical one is to him equivalent to supernaturalism." [10] It was this aspect of logical analysis which spawned logical empiricism and gained for this view the designation "positivistic." By virtue of its assumptions, logical empiricism presents an almost insuperable epistemological roadblock. Because language is conceived to be the only means by which thought can be articulated, and because whatever cannot be put into discursive, propositional form is relegated to the sphere of *feeling*, logical empiricism has drastically limited not only the knowable, but also what we already know, to what can be projected in discourse. The inarticulate discomfort of such a drastic limitation of the cognitive function was experienced among the more classical philosophers as well as those who were less technically competent to debate the philosophical issues involved.

If logical empiricism was invulnerable to attack on the ground of its reasoning — as *logicians* its proponents are unsurpassed — it would be senseless to waste ammunition in this direction. A more fruitful line of assault lay in the direction of its psychological bases. A telling advance was made in this direction by Susanne Langer in her *Philosophy in a New Key*,[11] the subtitle of which was *A Study in the Symbolism of Reason*,

Rite and Art. Thoroughly familiar with the work of Wittgenstein, Russell, and Carnap, Mrs. Langer had been influenced markedly by another philosophical tendency which had developed via Ernst Cassirer (1874–1945).

Whereas the work of the Vienna Circle, as well as that of Lord Russell, had been under the influence of the rapid advances made in natural science, mathematics as the language of natural science, and the logic of that language, Cassirer's inquiries had taken him into the areas of social psychology and cultural anthropology. Hence while the Vienna Circle strove toward a univocal language in which logical thought could be prosecuted, Cassirer was making a valiant effort to understand why and how concepts are born and framed by the human mind. Thus in this epoch-making book, Mrs. Langer was able to bring into coalescence two streams of thought which had developed somewhat independently. The result was considerably more than the sum of what went into it.

Because it could not or, perhaps, would not do so, empirical philosophy left the inquiry into the meaning of myth, ritual, and art to post-Kantian idealism, while it restricted its own inquiry more and more to the significance of the growing accumulation of natural scientific knowledge. The observations brought to the fore in the pursuit of what might be called the "mental sciences," particularly psychology and cultural anthropology, suggested to those philosophers attempting generalizations from this material that all mental activity begins in some sort of *symbolic transformation.* Consequently, the philosophy of symbolic form which grew out of these inquiries disclosed a loose foundation stone in the edifice constructed by empirical philosophers. As applied to logical empiricism, this observation pointed out that the error here was its failure to recognize that even its discursive propositions were the result of a process of symbolic transformation. Here the psychologist of language could be called upon to testify that an important step in the mental formulation of sense data had been overlooked by logical empiricism probably because, as philos-

ophers, they understood a great deal more about the behavior
of discursive propositions than the behavior of the beings who
devise them. A logical empiricist might readily admit this by
indicating that he was concerned with philosophy, which is
logic and epistemology for him, rather than with psychology,
which is a science and therefore only a part of a much larger
whole out of which he derives his data.

It should be emphasized, however, that in bringing together
the empirical and symbolist streams of thinking, Mrs. Langer
was not deserting that primary interest in logic which had
drawn her in the first place to Wittgenstein's *Tractatus
Logico-Philosophicus*.[12] She herself says that her essay
" spring[s] from logical rather than from ethical or metaphysical interests." [13] In probing the area that lies behind the propositions with which logical analysts are so thoroughly occupied,
her inquiry is directed toward exposing the logical structures
that underlie the various types of meaning situations; one of
these modes of symbolism is language, but equal attention is
also given to ritual, myth, and music. These latter are distinguished from language proper on the basis of their being
"nondiscursive" or "presentational." In the attempt to conceive all thought and knowledge as proceeding from " symbolic
transformation " and becoming discursive only at a later stage
in its formulation, the philosophy of symbolic form has taken
a seven-league step over the wall built around the knowable
by logical empiricism.

Even more important, perhaps, than discovering the Achilles'
heel of logisticizing philosophy is Mrs. Langer's conception of
the role played in the totality of human cerebration by the
function of symbolizing. In what amounts to an affirmation of
faith, she attributes this process to a need that is so characteristic of man that it can be said to distinguish him from the rest
of the animal world. In language that is more than faintly
reminiscent of the philosophy of organism, she characterizes
this need as an emergent that has but recently appeared in the
evolutionary process. The function of symbolizing, which re-

sponds to a need unique in man, goes on unceasingly despite the fact that its results, even in the majority of cases, may not eventuate in particularly useful concepts. Here we can see most clearly that the philosophy of symbolic form has arisen from the studies of the most normal activities of the human organism rather than from an exclusive attention to the natural sciences. For this very reason, the philosophy of symbolic form could act, in our present culture, as the clearinghouse of meaning, a function that Paul Tillich feels to be so urgently needed but so inadequately discharged by the logical analysts.[14]

One of the distinguishing marks of the philosophy of symbolic form is the attention it has paid to development in the field of psychology. It is quite apparent that this school of thought depends to a considerable extent for its scientific understanding of human mental activity upon Gestalt psychology. This newer psychological approach is to be distinguished from the earlier behaviorist schools as holism is to be distinguished from atomism. The name *Gestalt* is a German word meaning "form, configuration"; one of the basic tenets of the Gestalt psychologist is that the mind exhibits certain form-building characteristics that make it possible for the experient to organize his experience. From this viewpoint comes the Gestalt psychologist's critique of behaviorism and the other purely analytic approaches that tended to reduce psychology to the model of the natural sciences. To the Gestalt psychologist, the whole fabric of experience as it is organized in the human mind is more than the sum of the individual sense impressions which go to make it up; consequently, the Gestalt psychologist is not limited to observing and classifying the pure sensations that the atomistic psychologists consider the only proper area of inquiry.[15]

By way of corroboration of the essential contribution made by Gestalt psychology to an understanding of what is peculiarly human about the activity of perception and its organization into concepts, we may glance for a moment at another very young field of inquiry, cybernetics. In developing machines for

reproducing mental processes such as electronic variable auto-
matic computers and complex control apparatus employing
the principles of the servomechanism, cyberneticists were required to reproduce the results if not the actual processes of
the human mind. For more than a century, scientists had been
engaged in the development of a logical machine that, when
fed all sorts of data, could produce by deductive processes the
myriad possible correlations among them. This type of machine
could be made to learn by incorporating into the memory unit
certain corrections that were fed back from the results of its
actions. Thus, an adaptive or inductive machine was devised
by means of which another of the human mental activities
could be reproduced. This second type of machine, whose pro-
totype was Watt's governor applied to a steam engine, is what
controls the manufacture of standard products in an increasing
number of industries. The eradication of possible human error
in both the deductive and the inductive types of machines has
accounted for the phenomenal rise in efficiency ultimately responsible for mass production, but at the same time it has given
rise to fears of what all industrial workers know as automation.
The type of machine that yet exceeds the grasp of cybernetics
is one that, in the words of Jacob Bronowski, would " base
foresight on insight." [16] That is to say, it would be able, by conceptual reasoning or symbolizing, to perceive likenesses where
no likenesses were to be expected. The reason why such a machine is likely to remain an impossibility for a very long time
to come is simply that this process of symbolizing, this act of
symbolic transformation, is the *human* characteristic of *mind*.

Despite the idealistic tendencies that are to be detected in
Cassirer as a result of his own prior associations, his willingness
to come to terms with *emergence* as a distinguishing characteristic of the natural process has helped to make his philosophical viewpoint a necessary corrective to the almost completely mechanistic thought represented in logical empiricism.
As a Gestalt psychologist is prepared to step off the bank of
regularity into the complex and often confused world of per-

ception, wherein language plays a far too important role to be eliminated or consigned to the category of noise, so has the philosophy of symbolic form been adventurous enough to search the almost trackless jungle of symbolic activity which is so characteristic of mental activity in the recently emergent Homo sapiens. At the same time, this philosophic school has attempted to come to terms with the peculiarly social characteristics of the human animal. Here again, while language is of importance in such an inquiry, it is no less important that the symbolic forms whereby communal experience is organized and transmitted be examined as the bearer of meaning in social context. Thus, the organismic character of human society as demonstrated by cultural anthropology is coupled with an informed doctrine of evolution which is acquired from biological study, and the whole is generalized into a philosophical quest for meaning inside language and the means by which it is produced. The value of such an inquiry for the more adequate appreciation of the ultimate value of mythic expression will become more evident as we press our own penetration into the peculiar qualities of the Christian proclamation.

D. The Philosophy of Existence

However cursorily one reads the works of those philosophical schools with which we have been concerned up to this point, he cannot fail to be impressed by the predominance of rationalism and the almost exclusive preoccupation with what can be known about reality. The philosophies that we have scanned tend to treat man as an observer. Although it is true to a less extent of the philosophy of symbolic form, it can be said that logical empiricism conceives man as a totally detached mental observer of an exterior world and consigns whatever concerns him as a result of his uniquely human existence to an area called "feeling." Whether or not it is intended by these fundamentally scientific observers, the labeling of this area as "feeling" cannot avoid the pejorative significance of the term. Whether the philosopher is an empiricist for whom external objects are the primary, or even the only, source of knowledge or an idealist for whom the mind plays a unique role in imposing form on a formless world or perceiving the form within the phenomenal world, most representatives of the schools we have looked at are concerned primarily with epistemology. This situation only underlines the indebtedness of modern philosophy to Descartes (1596–1650) and indicates the more clearly the decisiveness of his contribution to thought since the seventeenth century. One of the most important results of the Cartesian cleavage between interior and exterior worlds, that is, between subject and object, has been the sundering of man from the natural world in which he exists. On the one hand, this has produced a radical division between nature and history; thus, there is a line of thought in which only the former is open to inquiry of lasting value. On the other hand, when the radical division is overcome, the attempt too frequently suffers from the original sundering so that man is reduced to the status of an object within the physical world from which he had previously been detached. In either case, the Cartesian shadow shuts out a good deal of light from the scene of human activity.

Slightly more than a century ago, a prophetic voice was raised and a protest registered against the exclusively rationalist approach to man and his place in the world. Sören Kierkegaard (1813–1855) developed his lone revolt not in the coolly analytic terms of an observer but in the passionate confessions of a man intimately involved in life and its ambiguities. Thinking and writing in the philosophical climate of the mid-nineteenth century, Kierkegaard gave vivid expression to the tension that is felt between *being* someone and *knowing about* something. Through his introspective, and to a considerable extent, autobiographical writings, he attempted to come to grips with the simple fact that his own existence is not a question for speculation but a process in which he is *involved*. In order to encounter existence, he says, it is necessary not to search one's mind for a reflection of it but to plunge into life.

The contrast is thus sharply drawn between *detachment,* which is the role of the observer, and *involvement,* which is the role of the man who would encounter himself and his existence. In its own unsystematic way, this is a challenge to the Cartesian cleavage, but it is also indicative of a challenge to Western philosophy's gradual but nonetheless certain flight from the question of Being.

Kierkegaard challenged the radical idealism of Hegel, whose thought dominated European philosophy in the nineteenth century and through European philosophy dominated the theology of the Lutheran Church of which Kierkegaard was a member. Hegel's identification of the real with the rational was the logical outcome of the development of European philosophical thought since the days of the Greeks. The attack mounted by Kierkegaard was, therefore, much more than a local skirmish; it was intended to shake the foundation of philosophical thought, but in Kierkegaard's mind the real reason for the shaking of these foundations was to break the hold of Hegelianism over Christian theology. He was far less interested in the reform of philosophy than he was in the freedom of the Christian faith to speak to man's real condition. To the extent that this undertaking involved him in philosophy, he was sharply critical of idealism, but he was primarily a religious writer rather than a critical philosopher.

It remained the task of a more systematic thinker to work out the implications of Kierkegaard's challenge and to develop a philosophical critique of idealism. Such a thinker was Martin Heidegger (1889–   ), who is likely to be recorded by future generations as one of the most seminal thinkers of the twentieth century. Previously to Heidegger, the academic world of philosophy could shrug off the questions raised by Kierkegaard and even those raised by the other great rebel, Friedrich Nietzsche (1844–1900). The ground for such indifference was simply that men like Kierkegaard and Nietzsche were primarily literary figures, poets and not professors. When Heidegger came onto the scene, however, academic philosophy was shaken by a professional philosopher whose technical competence could not be denied. Associated with Edmund Husserl at Freiburg from 1915 to 1923, Heidegger absorbed much from the founder of phenomenology and occupant of the chair of philosophy from 1916 to 1929. After six years during which he was Professor of Philosophy at Marburg, he was called back to Freiburg to succeed Husserl. Some four years later, he was elected rector of the university, and after slightly more than a year in this position under the National Socialist regime he retired to a village in the Black Forest.

Although a great deal of attention has been given to the more sensational side of Heidegger's thought and particularly to his contributions toward the better-known existentialists, the real contribution made by this great thinker lies in his critique of the whole philosophical inquiry since the classical Greek period. In this effort, Heidegger's debt to Husserl's method of phenomenology is most evident. The purpose of his most important work, *Sein und Zeit* (*Being and Time*), written and published before 1928, was an analysis of the meaning of " Being " and its relation to finitude. It is unfortunate that this most significant work was published only in incomplete form. As he conceived the work originally, it was to consist of two parts, the first analyzing the basic categories of ontological thought from the viewpoint of *what it means to be;* the second part was to be an outline description of the history of Western philosophy which would amount to nothing less than the complete destruction of the way in which this philosophical tradition had approached the question of Being. This second part has never been published, and only two of the projected three sections of the first part have appeared. Nevertheless, as one reads his essays and lectures in the light of the avowed purpose of *Being and Time,* it becomes quite clear what the main lines of the second part of that work are meant to be. The fact that his greatest contribution to philosophy has to be reconstructed and synthesized from his more recent problematic studies makes Heidegger rather difficult to follow; this also means that it is possible to quote him extensively in support of a position to which he would hardly subscribe. The fragmentary character of his published works may account for his being accredited with more than he would desire in the case of the more systematic and extant works of the existentialists.

The primary reason for Heidegger's being misunderstood or not adequately understood by his contemporaries and successors is to be found in his almost impossible German. It is difficult enough for one conversant with German to comprehend Heidegger's thought, but it approaches the impossible to try to render his German into another tongue. This characteristic is not due, however, to a desire on Heidegger's part to be obscurantic. It arises because he is convinced of the inadequacy of the traditional vocabulary of philosophy to convey the real problems in order that they might be recognized as problems and dealt with. Not only does he employ a vast number of unique German words, but he also reaches into the German vocabulary to use words not normally found in the philosophical vocabulary. This is part of his technique of analyzing the problems with which he considers philosophy to be primarily concerned. At the same time, he examines almost exhaustively the philology of the Greek terms in which the problem of Being has been posed and discussed for centuries.

Some critics of the philosophic tradition that has developed in Europe and America would trace the eclipse of ontology (that branch of philosophy which is occupied with the question of Being) by epistemology within that tradition to Immanuel Kant (1724–1804). These critics would appear to be right to the extent that both logical empiricism and existentialism, two of the leading movements in the West today, interpret in diametrically opposite ways Kant's dictum, "'Being' is obviously not a real predicate." [17] Nevertheless, the origin of modern preoccupation with epistemology is due, at least indirectly, to Descartes since Kant's dictum was made in the context of a critique of the Cartesian acceptance of the ontological argument for the existence of God.[18]

Heidegger's program took him to the roots of Greek thought in which the problem of Being, as he sees it, was formulated in such a way that succeeding centuries simply had to construe the problem in terms of epistemology. Consequently, he would search for the reason for the virtual disappearance of the problem of Being from Western thought in that period between the pre-Socratics and Aristotle. What he proposes is that the entire stream of ontological thinking, from the pre-Socratics onward, be studied phenomenologically, allowing this train of thought to be seen as it is without imposing upon it any prefabricated conceptions. It is his contention that the problem of Being receded and began its decline into oblivion with Plato's *Republic*. In the allegory of the cave (*Republic* VII. 1 ff.), Heidegger discovers a shift in the idea of *truth;* from that point onward, classical philosophy *detached* objects from their surroundings and construed truth as consisting in the correspondence of the intellectual perception of the object to the object that is being perceived. It is this act of detaching the object from its ground that Heidegger feels a strong impulse to reverse. Here we can see once more how Gestalt psychology is reflected; in speaking of objects and their context or surrounding, Gestalt psychology has made the terms "figure" and "ground" into technical terms. The tendency toward holistic thinking is thus underlined once more.

What many a modern critic of philosophical thought has been able to trace through Kant to Descartes, Heidegger appears to have tracked to the cave of Plato. He would readily grant that it was this act of detaching objects from their ground which has made possible the great scientific progress which is characteristic of the world that inherited classical philosophy. *Abstraction* (separation, disengagement) is the key to scientific study and to analytic progress, but the trouble begins when this utilitarian and secondary enterprise is made primary in the search for meaning. The point at which abstraction works its real havoc, according to Heidegger, is in detaching the human being from his ground. Human existence, which he designates *Dasein* (being-there), is best understood by resorting to a scientific analogy, which is not Heidegger's way of explaining it.

Anyone who has ever dealt with electricity or magnetism is familiar with a field of force. Unlike our conception of a body as enclosed within definable boundaries, a notion that is due ultimately to Newtonian physics, a field has no boundaries; that is to say, there is no line that can be described on one side of which attraction is operative and on the other side of which it is not. In a field of force, there is a center of intensity, and the intensity decreases in proportion to the distance from that center. This is a viable analogue of the way in which Heidegger conceives *Dasein*. To abstract a man from the field or ground of Being as an object or a subject (that is, as a body) is to deprive him of what is peculiar to his existence. A vital and most significant part of that field of Being includes what rationalism has dropped from consideration in its attempt to understand Being; such concerns as death, fear, anxiety, and despair are so rudimentary to an understanding of Being that Heidegger attempts to expound the peculiarly human quality of existence in terms both of its negative aspects and its positive aspects. His contrast between the Being of a " utensil " and the Being that is human leads him to a discussion of authentic and inauthentic Being.

Without delving more deeply into Heidegger's unfinished ontology, we can perceive that he is at pains to grasp systematically what it means *to be*. In the train of Heidegger, which can trace its ancestry back through Kierkegaard, there has dawned again upon the philosophical horizon a philosophy of existence which affirms what has apparently been forgotten if not purposely suppressed: " *that* I am " is at least as significant as " *what* I am," or differently put, Being is at least as vital for the quest of ultimate meaning as " quiddity." Into Heidegger's thought have appeared those aspects of reality which are not reducible to the clear and distinct language of scientific formulation.

As an expression of a philosophical viewpoint, however, the philosophy of existence has had a curious history in the last century. From the remote recesses of Christian theology, a rebellious voice was raised by one who faced the ambiguity of life in concrete decision (Kierkegaard); his protest was raised against the iron bands restricting the Christian faith in the name of idealism and its abstractness (Hegel). A philosophical giant (Heidegger) took up the protest, broadened and deepened it, and showed that it was as old as Greek thought. A professional philosopher (Karl Jaspers) recognized the validity of the protest, and in the course of recasting the terms in which the alternatives were posed, he expounded a philosopher's faith. Thus was raised again a philosophical question that had occupied thinkers at various points in history since the fifth century B.C.; Socrates knew the problem, Augustine had experienced it, and Pascal had lived in and through it.

It took the Enlightenment to bring the problem of Being to focus, however, because against that dazzling and sparkling background the opaqueness of the problem was the more evident. Rationalism might bask in the light on the other side of the problem, but the shadow cast by it could not be avoided by those whose perspective included the foreground of the picture as well as the background. Nor will the question of Being, what it means *to be* in the world, be silenced even now. Its persistent attraction is felt in all areas of human expression even more acutely in an age whose ambiguities cannot be obscured. Gabriel Marcel and Jean-Paul Sartre, Martin Buber and Nicolas Berdyaev, each from his own vantage point and out of his own peculiar experience, have grappled with the question which will not let them go. The literary productions of our era likewise reiterate what painters and sculptors express in their own peculiar media. Shakespeare's young prince of Denmark is echoed by the Danish Lutheran zealot, and the chorus of voices has even penetrated the isolation of the philosopher's study in the midst of ivy-covered academic halls.

All of this attention directed toward so vital a reality as

Being cannot help being reflected in the language of philosophy and theology. This is particularly true in English since the word " being " is patient of several interpretations. First of all, it is a participle, but it is also a gerund; thus it may be used both as adjective and as noun. There are further confusions, however, since to use it as an adjective permits a further use as noun. In the same way as one may say " *the good* die young," he may also say " man is *the being* who knows when he is well off." The substantive use of the adjective " being " is actually shorthand for " one who is." If we desire to name the fact *that he is,* we may do so by the infinitive form " to be " or the gerund form " being " ; this fact is amply demonstrated by the virtual identity of the two utterances, " *to be* is better than *to know* " and " *being* is better than *knowing.*" The confusion that arises in English between the gerund " being " and the participle " being " stems from the stylistic rules of English prose that prevent us from substituting the infinitive form for the gerund in many cases. Consequently, to reduce this confusion to a minimum, writers of theological and philosophical treatises in English have adopted the convention of writing " being " when they mean the participle and " Being " when they mean the gerund.

There is a further ambiguity in the use of the verb " to be " which is encountered in many translated works which deal in ontology. The infinitive " to be " may be replaced by the gerund " Being," but it is frequently replaced by the noun " existence." The difficulty inherent in the use of the noun " existence " comes from its various possible meanings in English. It may be used pejoratively to make a contrast with the fuller life; this is evident when a wit may offer as a judgment of a dull life, " His is no life; it's an existence! " As we have already suggested, it may be used as the rough equivalent of " to be." When the German word *Dasein* (*da,* " there, here," *sein,* " to be ") is rendered into English, it is frequently, if not consistently, translated by the noun " existence." There is another meaning for the noun " existence," which, by virtue of its etymology, is rich in depth. Heidegger has pointed out that this word is a virtual equivalent of " self-transcendence " since it comes from the Latin verb *exsisto* (*ex*, " out," *sisto*, " cause to stand ") which can mean " emerge." Consequently, the term " existence " can point to a higher or more authentic mode of Being. Because some writers are less careful than others, they may cause confusion by their use of the word " existence " or some form of it; even if the writer is careful, however, the reader may not follow the distinctions.

While it is to be welcomed that philosophy is taking more seriously a problem that has been in abeyance for a considerable period of time, one cannot avoid the fact that this new direction of thought will make certain inordinate demands upon our language. These demands will, in turn, result in other demands upon writers and readers alike for serious attention to accuracy of expression. The gain in scope will not be achieved without a certain amount of pain, for a language does not alter course as easily as a sloop comes about when the wind direction demands it.

In confining our attention to three philosophical trends in the current scene, we have attempted to see what philosophy is saying about language. By limiting ourselves to linguistic analysis, the philosophy of symbolic form, and the philosophy of existence, we have concentrated upon those philosophical inquiries in which language plays a leading role. This was especially evident in the first two, and indirectly clear in connection with the last named. Nevertheless both symbolic transformation and the emphasis upon Being are an implied critique of logisticizing philosophy. The problem of Being, however, seems to be a " family problem " confined almost exclusively to the language group in which the most significant advances in the study of ontology have been made. Linguistic philosophy would look entirely different were it to be pursued in the Semitic languages or in one of the other language groups about which we know so very little. This observation is a product of a relatively new science known as linguistics; its contributions toward our search for a language for Christian communication will bear closer examination. Consequently, we should listen to what the scientist of human expression, the linguist, has to say about the phenomenon over which so much philosophizing has taken place in our generation.

Chapter III

Language and Meaning:
Linguistics and Semantics

Language, speech, and communication cover a wide range of phenomena which have occupied scholars, scientists, and educators with increasing emphasis in the past few decades. So diverse are the phenomena, despite their apparent unity through language, that it was to be expected that a number of independent fields of study would arise. Frequently, these new and independent fields were so concerned with the immediate problems they set out to examine that they were unaware of the beginnings which had been made in one line or another of previous inquiry. In some instances, of course, co-operation was well-nigh impossible since the novelty of the field and its interest precluded it; in other cases, co-operation has been secured among fields of inquiry which at first sight might seem to have little in common, e.g., the clinical treatment of aphasia and the science of physics. Obviously, psychology is vastly interested in all the dimensions of speech, language, and communication; remote as it may seem at the moment, a psychology of language is at least a possibility.

As specialization increases in a scientific period, it becomes increasingly difficult to maintain lines of communication even among psychologists themselves, let alone between psychologists and other scientists. Conferences on communication theory and information retrieval are a step in this direction, but practical interests seem to override the drive toward theoretical generalization. Each of the particular areas of specialization in psychology leads to a field of inquiry that is outside the field of psychology proper, and thus the psychologist concerned with language is drawn in two directions at once. His own inquiries may be of invaluable assistance to a physicist or a philologist, but the barriers between them are detrimental to the development of each other's theory as well as to the achievement of a total or general view.

One of the most important problems facing those who are engaged in the study of one aspect or another of language is that of achieving a greater degree of unity and co-operation among the various specialties in order that duplication may be eliminated and certain problems dealt with more accurately through closer communication. How broad the field of language study is in its present condition may be gathered from a report published a few years ago at the request of the Carnegie Corporation.[19] This report demonstrates how many different types of inquiry are now being pursued under the general heading of language. It also underlines the need for closer communication among psychologists, linguists, educators, philosophers, and social scientists.

What is becoming more evident is the need for a science of communication, but such a science is still far from an actuality. Until there is greater interest in the educational field for raising up that kind of *generally educated theorist* who is sufficiently aware of the general outreach of the social and natural sciences as well as of the humanities to gather the threads together into a generalized view, we shall have to depend upon the fragmentary communication among specialists to illuminate what other specialists are doing. This means, of course, that our understanding of communication will frequently be based upon a rather myopic view of the technical problems involved in language as a human phenomenon. In turn, the way in which language is understood and taught will have a marked influence upon our general comprehension of the magnitude of the problem of language as it relates to philosophy and theology. As we have already noticed, modern philosophy is profoundly concerned, in one way or another, with language both as a conceptual tool and as a means of communication. In the center of this matrix of problems stands the problem of meaning, and the approach to it will again be determined by some preconceptions as to what meaning involves. These preconceptions arise from the science of communication that is implicit in our present fragmented way of looking at the problem of language.

The plan of the present chapter is to set linguistic science in its proper context. Then, since the semantic problem is almost *the* problem of language in our day, we shall look at semantics as a field of inquiry. This survey will lead us inevitably to one of the most vital aspects of the problem of meaning as it relates to the peculiar problem of Christian communication.

A. Linguistics and Language

During the present century, we have seen something resembling a Copernican revolution in the study of languages and language. We can account for the method of observation and the organization of those observations peculiar to psychological studies of language because these disciplines view human speech from the vantage point of modern scientific method. Psychology reflects the development of scientific method on the model of the natural sciences. To a vast number of psychologists, language is a natural phenomenon and can be treated more or less mechanically. In a very important sense, psychology is a relative newcomer to the field of scholarly study, and it grew up under the aegis of the natural sciences, attempting to vindicate itself by the use of methods acceptable to other scientists. On the other hand, the study of language as a cultural phenomenon — the accumulation and organization of lexical data, the classification of inflectional features, the systematic explanation of the rules of syntax, and more recently the gathering and systematizing of phonological data — is an old inhabitant of the scholarly scene.

By the middle of the second century B.C., Aristarchus (ca.

216-144) and isolated and described the ancient dialect of the Greek language in which the *Iliad* and the *Odyssey* were composed. During the second century A.D., Herodian composed some thirty-three monographic epitomizing the grammatical studies of his predecessors and incorporating his own observations particularly on the subjects of accentuation and inflection. Because the classical Greek written by the Athenians during the fourth century B.C. assumed in the Hellenistic age the proportions of an ideal form of discourse, Hellenistic grammarians concentrated their attention upon its structure and produced numerous studies of its manifold characteristics.

Until quite recently in the history of academic inquiry, the study of languages was confined almost totally to the humanities. One clear index to the status of language as a subject for inquiry is the structure of a university faculty. The grammar and literature of a single tongue, or a closely related group of tongues, has been the domain for which separate language departments have been responsible: Germanic Languages and Literature, Romance Languages and Literature, Classical Languages and Literature, etc. The fundamental reason for this structure of the university faculty has been that each language or language group won its way into the university curriculum, only after considerable struggle. In the medieval university (*studium generale*), there was only one language and that was Latin. Other languages were added to the curriculum, but the structure of the course of study was dictated by the conception of encyclopedia which governed medieval learning; hence, new languages were added piecemeal, and the study of them was never integrated into the over-all structure of the course of study.

There was another reason for this situation growing out of the medieval background of seventeenth-century European universities. This is known as the *philological* approach to the study of language. As that term is used in Europe, it applies to "the study of the specific culture of one nation."[20] The philological approach to the study of a given language treats that language primarily, almost exclusively, as a tool for getting at the cultural ideas assumed to be in the literature of that speech community. Only enough of the *language* in question is studied to permit the student to read the literature of the people whose language it is; frequently, after a brief introduction to the peculiarities of the language, a considerable amount of the literature is read in translation. This means that specific languages, or even groups of languages are not studied for themselves as a system of symbols; it also means that the entire spread of language from Greek to the Papuan dialects is left out of the average liberal arts curriculum. Beneath all of this, of course, lies an implicit assumption that the problems inherent in the outlook of any speech community can be appreciated and perhaps even dealt with apart from any firsthand association with the language itself.

The impetus to a scientific study of language came from the discovery of the meticulous, descriptive work done by the Hindu grammarians. From the nineteenth century onward, the philological approach to language gradually gave way to the historical study of language as an essential aspect of linguistic studies. During the preceding century, Johann Gottfried Herder had proposed that language had a natural rather than a divine origin, and his view was shared by a number of other thinkers including Rousseau. Although these men were not primarily linguists, in the technical sense, they did pave the way for the development of a scientific study of language. The main obstacle to be overcome in this movement toward a more objective approach to the relationships among various languages was the tacit assumption that all languages stemmed from a common ancestor. Related to this obstacle was another assumption, that all philosophical problems relating to language could be solved by recourse to more precise study of Latin and Greek, and more particularly the latter.

It was only natural that medieval humanistic studies should see the problem of language almost exclusively in terms of the Greek and Roman idiom. From the fifth century until the sixteenth, all learning was prosecuted in the Latin tongue which had been modified sufficiently to mediate the essentially Greek ideas which underlay medieval thought. Practically no Greek was known in the West until comparatively late in this period; as for Hebrew, it would seem that whatever opportunities for closer touch with the language presented themselves, they were missed or purposely avoided in the Middle Ages. The rise of the vernacular tongues in Europe created a cleavage between the learned and the illiterate. This cleavage was only partially overcome when the European universities, at a comparatively recent date, were forced to offer lectures in the vernacular tongues. The invention of printing hastened the eclipse of Latin as the only tongue in which academic discourse was carried on, but Latin had left an indelible imprint upon the study of vernacular tongues. Latin grammar was the model upon which all grammars of European languages were originally constructed, and even today in our own country, this imprint is visible in the grammars and introductory books used in the teaching of foreign languages. The superimposition of the categories of Latin Grammar upon English is one stubborn remnant of this effect, and the teaching of classical rhetoric is another.

When the Renaissance gave way to the Age of Discovery and and the Age of Imperialism, those who journeyed to the far reaches of the globe were far less interested in the new and strange languages they heard than they were in the goods and materials which could be extracted from the exotic new lands and the heathen illiterate who spoke these incomprehensible tongues. What interest they had in these languages was purely practical, although the practical interest was to bear unexpected fruit in the days to come. Scholars and observers were a dispensable luxury to this rough and ready band of traders and explorers. Had they been able to afford them, and had they wanted them, it is highly unlikely that these scholars would have contributed much to an understanding of these languages because of their preoccupation with the languages of Europe as the "languages of civilization." It was a long time before even modest beginnings were made toward accurate analysis of the languages encountered in the new regions opened to European scrutiny.

Some of the Christian missionaries who followed in the wake of the pioneers did make an effort to understand the languages of the newly acquired lands, but they were hampered not only by their lack of linguistic perception but by a conflict of ultimate aims as well. The official policy with respect to natives of these far-off lands rarely expressed a Christian attitude; all too frequently the missionary enterprise was directed toward the spread of European culture rather than the cultivation of an indigenous Christianity. Then too, the zeal of many of the missionaries, if not all of them, far outran their competence to deal with new and altogether strange tongues. The missionaries had been educated in a European atmosphere, and they reflected a European attitude toward language; consequently, they could not be expected to give a descriptive account of these languages as they existed, even if they had been better educated. Since the chief purpose of penetrating these tongues was the translation of the Christian gospel as the missionaries knew it, their translations frequently reflected the cultural accretions of European Christianity undistinguished from the central affirmations of the gospel.[21] When the new languages were discovered to be inadequate to carry these strictly European characteristics, the immediate judgment was that the language must be primitive. That judgment reflected the attitude of language study in the nations whence these missionaries came in the seventeenth and eighteenth centuries.

Two separate lines of inquiry coalesced to form what is currently known as linguistic science. One of these was an effort that had gone on in Europe with reference to the European tongues themselves, and the other was a relatively new enterprise undertaken as a part of cultural anthropology. The linguistic studies of Franz Bopp (1791–1867), Jacob Grimm (1785–1863), and Rasmus Rask (1787–1832) prepared the way for later work by Berthold Delbrück (1842–1922) in Germanics and in other scholarly examinations of various groups of European languages. One of the major difficulties that hampered a large segment of nineteenth-century linguistics was a tendency to develop theories of linguistic change based upon inadequate observation; the theories derived by these scholars through the method of generalization applied to *European* languages. This does not mean that such generalizations might not hold for other language families, but beneath many of these generalizations lurked the assumption that whatever applied to Indo-European languages applied to all languages.

Alongside the work mentioned, and in part independent of it, a responsible science of descriptive linguistics was growing, however slowly. Otto von Böhtlingk (1815–1904), Friedrich Müller (1834–1898), and Franz Finck (1867–1910) all had delved into languages that were unrelated to Indo-European languages. They had to *describe* these languages before they could draw any theoretical generalizations about syntax, lexicology, or phonology; no historical backlog of grammatical theory lay at hand for their use as a guide. This procedure of studying language reached its epitome in the posthumously published works of Ferdinand de Saussure (1857–1913), who is generally recognized as the father of modern linguistic science. All modern linguistic scientists accept in general a dictum of his that descriptive studies precede historical studies and both precede comparative studies. Thus linguistic science now proceeds upon a principle that, in effect, reverses the actual direction taken by linguistic studies as they developed into linguistic science.

Meanwhile, the cultural anthropologists had begun to penetrate the various civilizations that had grown to different levels of maturity outside the orbit of European hegemony. Together with archaeologists and other specialists, these scholars are still probing the cultures of Southeast Asia, Africa, North and South America, the Pacific Islands, and various other areas including Australasia. Many of the languages spoken in these areas have never been reduced to writing, although it is clear that they have been spoken for periods of time that stretch back to the days before Europe's emergence from barbarian domination. A method had to be developed whereby these languages could be described and reduced to manageable medium. Adopting the methods employed by nineteenth-century students of non-European languages and adapting them to the new phenomena, linguistic anthropologists have come to understand even more clearly than did the missionaries of previous centuries that philosophical presuppositions imported from the study of Indo-European tongues were not only a hindrance in acquiring a knowledge of the non-European languages — these presuppositions actually prevented such knowledge. They came to an empirical judgment that many generalizations about language and its structure had been founded upon far too few observations of linguistic habits and of the languages themselves.

As it is currently practiced, linguistic science is a science; it is now carried on to a considerable extent, however, within the area which we call the social sciences. Like cultural anthropologists, linguistic scientists have to be somewhat amphibious. Both have a claim upon a place in the humanities — anthropology through ancient and modern history, linguistics through classical and modern languages — yet they are both forced to find a home elsewhere. The parent disciplines have rejected these newer offspring to a considerable extent, so that the science of linguistics has come to somewhat uncomfortable temporary rest among the social sciences. The study and teaching of modern languages such as French or German have provided a bridge over which linguistic science can enter into the humanities. For the most part, however, linguistic science has made no real impact upon the study of the classical languages. The method has been extremely helpful, on the other hand, for penetrating some of the lesser known Near Eastern tongues. Some reason for the lag in the effect upon the older disciplines may be found in the method of linguistic science.

The approach to any language, known or unknown, made by the linguistic scientist is phenomenological. Because of a recognition that a language is never static, that it is never uniform even during a given period, and that new experience is a powerful agent of modification, the linguistic scientist employs a primarily inductive method for gathering data and making classifications and tentative generalizations. His analysis of a given language is made in three different dimensions, which, for purposes of summary, we designate as functional, spatiotemporal, and structural. In the first dimension of the functional he distinguishes three basic areas of inquiry: phonology, lexicology, and syntax. Phonology deals with the store of distinctive sounds peculiar to the language being examined, i.e., its phonemes; lexicology covers the total collection of meaningful units belonging to the language, i.e., its words, including all the various inflectional and other shapes a meaningful unit may take; and syntax includes those relational complexes into which words normally enter when used in discourse, i.e., phrases, sentences, etc. As we know from our own language, however, a considerable difference in each of these functional aspects is to be found between any two periods in which the language is spoken, and we also know that there are dialect differences which are often quite as distinctive. This knowledge provides the second dimension of the analysis of all language according to linguistic science: the spatiotemporal. Thus, a language as it is spoken or written at a given point in its history within a geographical area is first of all described in categories of phonology, lexicology, and syntax. Several of these particular phases of the language may then be arranged chronologically or geographically in order to establish phonological, lexical, or syntactical change. The former enterprise is called descriptive linguistics and the latter, historical linguistics.

The force of de Saussure's dictum that descriptive analysis precedes historical analysis becomes quite apparent, especially as it applies to little-known languages. The utility of this approach for organizing the study of better-known languages is far from universally appreciated by students and teachers of those languages the study of which has been founded on less scientific bases. This feature is one of the primary reasons why linguistic scientists will rarely be found among those whose primary line of inquiry is in the languages which have formed the backbone of cultural studies for the past several centuries.

Linguistic scientists of more recent date than de Saussure have been able to make several improvements upon the model of linguistics as set forth by the great master. One of the important contributions made by this younger group of linguists is the addition of a third dimension to the study of language.[22] It is important to us since it affects *semantics,* which has been, for a long time, the stepchild of language study frequently inhabiting a corner of philosophy. Because meaning could possibly be limited to lexicology, the place of semantics in the model of linguistic science has been debated both inside the discipline and outside. It has been argued, however, with a good deal of cogency that meaning is as much a part of syntax as it is of lexicology; in fact, what are known as *idioms* provide an excellent instance of this fact. The simple question, "What's the matter?" is well understood in English-speaking communities; it cannot be translated into all of the Indo-European tongues, however, without resorting to some phrase or clause peculiar to that tongue. On the other hand, nothing less than a word carries meaning — even if it contains but one sound, it is still a word — so that phonology does not submit to semantic analysis.

The net result of these observations has been the addition of what is called the *structural* dimension to language study; its component parts are morphology and semantics. Therefore, each part of linguistic study has three dimensions: functional, spatiotemporal, and structural. The only exception to this rule is phonology, which has but two dimensions: functional and spatiotemporal, its structural dimension always being morphological.

Thus it is possible to divide the study of language into the following parts:

> *Phonology*
>> descriptive phonology
>> historical phonology
>
> *Lexicology*
>> descriptive lexical morphology
>> historical lexical morphology
>> descriptive lexical semantics
>> historical lexical semantics
>
> *Syntax*
>> descriptive syntactic morphology
>> historical syntactic morphology
>> descriptive syntactic semantics
>> historical syntactic semantics

The descriptive portions of this study are otherwise known as synchronistic, and the historical portions are similarly known as diachronistic. The former are always concerned with a given period and locale of the language while the latter are concerned with change. It was de Saussure's contention that change could be discussed only in relation to one of the functional aspects at a time, thus generalizations about language as a phenomenon were not really encouraged by his model of the science.

A further modification of the model of the science is still in the fluid stage of experiment while linguistic scientists attempt to work out its significance. This shift in direction involves the addition of a third division to the spatiotemporal dimension of the science. As we recall, the spatiotemporal dimension consisted of two aspects: the descriptive, a language at any given point, and the historical, several points connected temporally or spatially. By confining this dimension to the study of these two aspects, linguistic science seemed to be impeding progress toward more inclusive generalizations about linguistic behavior. So long as de Saussure's model was rigidly observed linguists could generalize only about a single tongue and its dialects. It was possible to draw away from this narrow line by treating several very similar languages as dialects of an assumed central tongue thus opening up the possibility of the grammar of a family of languages. Farther than this it was impossible to go, and many linguistic scientists are happy that this is the case. Yet some venturesome linguists are anxious to move beyond the borders to a more inclusive territory. That is to say, they wish to move from generalizations about specific languages and language families to language-in-general, if there is such a thing. At the moment, there are signs that an increasing number of linguistic scientists are prepared to make cautious, but firm, generalizations about phonological change as it applies to language-in-general; many, if not all, refuse to go farther.

The introduction of this new category, panchronistic linguistics, parallel to synchronistic and diachronistic linguistics, makes possible, although hardly probable in the immediately foreseeable future, an inductive philosophy of grammar as a viable substitute for the discredited deductive philosophies of grammar which were so common before the advent of linguistic science. This type of study would add five more branches of linguistics, but each of these five would have to proceed from its counterpart in the historical categories as each of the historical categories proceeds from the relevant descriptive categories. The most important contribution that could be made by this sort of study is a scientific foundation for the analysis of meaning. Semantics on a panchronistic level leading from the historical and descriptive study of meaning in a sufficiently large number of unrelated language families could provide a number of clues to help us out of some of the problems into which our wrangles about the philosophy of language have led us.

The possibilities of the field of panchronistic linguistics have hardly yet been visualized; the realization of even the simplest beginnings is hampered by the fact that discussion of this approach is extremely difficult of access. In the first place, most of the suggestions for such a field of study and its possibilities appear in monographic form in the dozen or so European periodicals devoted primarily to general linguistics. Since most of the articles are written in one or more of the European languages, access is somewhat difficult even if the periodicals were available and known about; very few scholars outside the field of general linguistics even know about these periodicals, much less read them. In the second and equally important place, these articles are written by and for practicing linguistic scientists; therefore, the terminology in which these seminal suggestions are couched provides a barrier surmountable only by one versed in the technical vocabulary of linguistic science. Nevertheless, the contributions that will be made in the future by the discipline of linguistics to the larger problem of communication will in considerable measure stem from this front.

One of the most important contributions of linguistic science to the problem of communication is that it offers another doorway by which language may once again approach philosophy. The philosophy that is known as logical empiricism, one of whose tributaries rises in the early development of descriptive linguistics, has commanded a large segment of the philosophic thought of the present because of its inherent critique of the aprioristic foundations of a great part of traditional philosophic thought. Because the Greeks knew no language other than their own, or at least considered no other language worth studying, it was quite normal that they should assume that there was some invariable correlation between the structure of their language and the universal forms of thought and cosmic order. Consequently, there was a high degree of correspondence between their formal grammar and their metaphysics. This is the point of an observation, made in another connection by Bertrand Russell and paraphrased by Mrs. Langer, to the effect that " the Aristotelian metaphysic of substance and attribute is a counterpart of the Aristotelian logic of subject and predicate." [23] The presupposition behind Greek philosophy in this regard was bequeathed to Western thought through idealism, but it was also operative in critiques of idealism, simply because they were *critiques* of idealism. In a very important sense, the logisticizing philosophers of our own day are caught in this web since they seem to be bound to a theory of definition that is part of the deductive system against which many of their most vehement protests are voiced.

Linguistic science may not yet have developed sufficiently to provide us with a blueprint for understanding the mental processes that have produced the great systematic philosophies of the world, yet its method of phenomenological study as applied to language ought to show us a pathway by which we can describe what we discover in the structure of unrelated languages. In this way, we shall be able to *listen* to what is peculiar to a given language before we try to impose upon its structure the logic of another language structure. This applies most clearly to Hebrew, and thus, in turn, provides a gateway to a clearer understanding of what the Christian gospel is all about *on its own ground*. An attempt will be made to apply these canons to the Christian proclamation in the following chapter.

Meanwhile, it is the very problem of meaning introduced by our discussion of semantics which leads us to a closer look at the science of meaning. This term has caused so much consternation that we should be well advised to get it into focus, and the point at which this should be done is at the intersection of linguistics and philosophy.

B. " It Is All a Matter of Semantics! "

Both the strength and the weakness of spoken as well as written language may be traced to the plurality of meaning attaching to many words and phrases in the vocabulary. A single set of sounds comprising one meaning unit can and frequently does convey a number of separate meanings not always related in readily determined ways. Although we may not be able to account in detail for the origin of any language, it is apparent from the evidence available that languages arose for quite practical purposes. When this medium was employed for more precise ends, such as science or philosophy, and for more expressive efforts, such as poetry and religion, the vocabulary and syntax of this medium were taxed heavily. Since speech sounds are quite arbitrary, the problem of meaning must involve the subject matter that is being formulated. Consequently, the problem of meaning takes us beyond the immediate province of language into the entire realm of human knowledge. Reflection upon the relation between the two, language and human knowledge, comprises the field known as semantics. Because it occupies so many scholars of such widely differing backgrounds, however, semantics is a field that to the casual observer appears to be hopelessly confusing. Certain rather definite divisions of responsibility are emerging from this somewhat confused picture, and if one is patient enough, he can discern the outline of a rather clear model in this field which is still in process of defining itself and articulating its aims and goals.

The immediate impression one gets upon reading a summary description of this field is one of utter terminological chaos. If any field could be expected to show some respect for terminological accuracy, it should be one dedicated to the study of meaning. Some of the language employed by semanticists appears to be a proper subject for semantic analysis. Part of the difficulty arises from the divergent interests of those who pursue the subject, but a larger part of the difficulty owes its existence to a lack of communication among the various groups during the early stages of growth of this study.

The problem is dramatized in the word "semantics," which is an ambiguous term. The word itself comes from the Greek, being a transliteration of a quite common Attic word; in form it is an adjective meaning " significant." Aristotle used it with a linguistic sense in describing a *noun* as a " sound significant (*sēmantikē*) by convention, having no reference to time, of which no portion is significant (*sēmantikon*) separate from the rest." [24] As a noun in form, "semantics" first appeared in a book review written in French by Gaston Paris [25]; his term, *la sémantique*, was used henceforth to designate the area of linguistics concerned with the signification of words. While linguistic science has been struggling to define the area covered by semantics, other scholars have been experimenting with terminology to define what they understand to be involved in the elusive concept of meaning.

As Ogden and Richards have so ably pointed out, "meaning" is a term so thoroughly overworked by philosophers, logicians, and psychologists that it is no longer usable in any precise way. [26] Because of the subtle ambiguities inherent in the word "meaning," it has been necessary to devise some generally accepted terminology to discriminate among the various senses in which the term is used. Although not all writers on the subject agree on a detailed terminology, enough consensus has been achieved so that the terms used by some semanticists can be translated into the terminology of others. Where general agreement has been achieved is in the matter of relation among three points in the conceptual process. Represented graphically, it is known as the "triangle of meaning." [27] The points are variously designated according to the writer involved. The diagram will help to clarify the meaning situation.

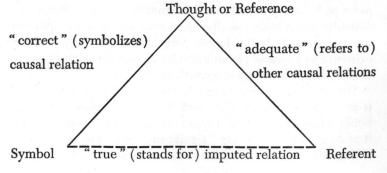

Thought or Reference

"correct" (symbolizes)   "adequate" (refers to)

causal relation   other causal relations

Symbol   "true" (stands for) imputed relation   Referent

Several inferences follow from this graphic representation of the meaning situation: (1) a symbol symbolizes a thought or reference; (2) a thought or reference refers to a referent; (3) it is not possible to proceed from referent to symbol without passing through the reference. Thus envisaged, the process of symbolizing is a two-stage operation, the broken line at the base of the triangle indicating the arbitrary relationship between the "thing meant" and the symbol used to indicate it. From this diagram, it is also possible now to clarify certain different meanings given to the word "semantics."

Linguistic semantics is concerned with the left side of the triangle. The manifold levels of relation between the symbol and the thought or reference is what a linguist who specializes in semantics understands as the specific area of his inquiry. By excluding the right side of the triangle, the linguistic scientist does not mean to deny the validity of investigations into the method of forming adequate thoughts about perceived reality; this area he is content to leave to psychology and epistemology. By the same token, his lack of immediate concern for the base of the triangle merely indicates that he is prepared to leave this area to the logician.

A complication has been introduced into linguistic semantics by the suggestion that this line of inquiry should be known as "semasiology." There are obvious advantages to this suggestion, not the least of which is that it would tend to put it in parallel with the other *structural* term "morphology," with which it is so closely related. As indicated in the previous section, there does not seem to be any real reason for differentiating so sharply between these two structural aspects on a terminological basis; the substitution of "semasiology" for "semantics" would reduce the confusion created by overworking an already difficult term. The objection to this suggestion comes chiefly from the French linguists who, perhaps patriotically, cling to the word popularized by Gaston Paris This objection is reinforced by a general tendency toward stability in a science that is yet in its infancy. Some linguistic semanticists use the suggested term while others reject it as a barbarism; nevertheless, the suggestion still remains meritorious.

As an indication of the ubiquity of the word "semantics" we need compare only two rather diverse, but clearly related, movements within the broad field rather imprecisely called philosophy. The growing concern with the weakness of ordinary language as a medium for precise logical expression gave rise some three decades ago to a movement for constructing an artificial language for logic. The roots of *symbolic logic* are to be traced back into the nineteenth century among theoretical mathematicians, but advances have been by leaps and bounds in these last few decades. As a part of this movement, a tendency to concentrate upon meaning was noticeable. The philosopher-scientists, led by the Polish logician Leon Chwisteck and aided by Rudolf Carnap and Alfred Tarski, developed a theoretical area designated "philosophical semantics," a branch of logic. The upshot of this development was Charles Morris' general theory of signs. Morris called this theory *semiotic* [28] (derived from the Greek word *sēmeiōsis*, "the act of indicating, noticing"), showing how recourse to Greek has brought new terms into the language in the attempt to clarify. His semiotic analysis consists of three dimensions:

1. Syntactics — the study of the purely formal relations of signs to one another. (Cf. the linguistic scientists' category of semantics carried under structure.)

2. Semantics — relation of signs to the objects they denote. (Cf. the base of the Ogden-Richards triangle.)

3. Pragmatics — science of relation of signs to their interpreters (opening psychology to philosophy).

Apart from the obvious terminological disagreements, it can be seen how the areas mapped out by Morris coincide roughly with those defined by linguistic semanticists. A philosophical semanticist is concerned with precisely the dimension, however, which the linguistic semanticist appears to exclude from his own studies.

A considerably different approach to the problem of meaning, undertaken first by Alfred Korzybski, has generated a school of thought which designates its enterprise by the rather misleading name "general semantics." The practitioners of this art are almost exclusively American, and a large majority of them are professionally involved in faculties of speech, departments of interpretation, and schools of public relations and communication. At its inception in the early thirties, general semantics was the attempt of its founder to bring all that he knew about semantics in its various aspects to bear upon a unified theory of education. When Korzybski wrote *Science and Sanity*,[29] he did not intend to set forth a new body of factual data but to reorient people's thinking, speaking, and listening so that they might communicate with one another effectively.

The foundations upon which Korzybski built his entire outlook included such widely diversified fields of knowledge as symbolic logic and depth psychology; between these poles he ranged at will across the various disciplines and into the very depths of them. One of his prime targets in every field into which he delved was the plethora of dogmas and assumptions which had apparently gone unchallenged for centuries. Each of the fields to which these dogmas and assumptions were attributed had exposed their untenability, but the general public seemed unaware of this.

Korzybski dedicated himself to making the new orientation, required by this scientific revolution, the ground of human discourse at its various levels. His studies in various disciplines into which he had gone demonstrated that the dominance of Aristotle was at an end; at the same time, he was well aware that Aristotle still held sway over the discourse of even the most educated conversants. By means of a few simple rules, he hoped to train people to *evaluate their own processes of valuation*. In the *use*, rather than the mere rote learning, of these basic rules, people's orientation could be changed from the *intensional*, based upon definitions of words in terms of words, to the *extensional*, based upon definitions of words and concepts according to the systematic organization of observed life facts.[30] This change in orientation, this release from the demonic power of words constituted for Korzybski not only a description of how the best scientific minds actually work but how all minds should operate. Thus envisaged, Korzybski's system amounted to an articulate theory of sanity in human beings.

Korzybski's principle of extensional orientation has also been characterized as an insistence upon *operational* definition of terms. The intensional type of definition, Aristotelian in origin, defines terms by way of classifying the concept or term and then differentiating the term from all other members of its class. This sort of definition makes entities out of concepts, and if it is not as carefully employed as Aristotle tried to do, it creates a world of unreality. The main difficulty of an intensional definition is that it does not really relate what is being defined to the experience of the person involved.

The purpose of the *operational* definition is to bridge this gap and to clarify what is really being talked about. The operational definition springs from a dynamic concept of reality and releases much of our thinking from the tyranny of words. The intensional definition has uses, but they are strictly limited. Therefore, even when it appears that an intensional definition is what is required, it can be phrased in such a way that it brings the hearer into closer relation to the objects of his own experience. An operational definition describes the operations that are to be performed or experienced so that whatever is being defined may be experientially participated in. Thus, definition is seen as a process involving both the discovery of the meaning of a question asked and relating the answer to the experience of the hearer. As a recent writer on the subject put it: " There can be no completely general rule for making definitions. The making of . . . definitions is an ' art ' rather than a ' science.' " [31]

In general semantics, the base of the Ogden-Richards triangle appears to be in the foreground again, but this is only an illusion. The concerns of the general semanticist are predominantly with the right side, the "adequacy" side, of the triangle, although he looks at the whole triangle in the process. The origin of the name " *general* semantics " may be attributed in part to its concern with the whole triangle, but it is more probably due to the fact that the viewpoint of general semantics applies equally to all phases of human activity in which language is involved. At all events, it seems to have made a general impression at the popular level which far exceeds anything accomplished in this regard by linguistic semantics or philosophical semantics.

One further confusion has recently been introduced into the use of the word "semantics." Certain linguistic scientists have suggested that what we characterized as panchronistic linguistics, in the preceding section, be called general linguistics; thus the area known as panchronistic semantics would become general semantics. At this point we begin to feel a certain sympathy for Seneca when he observed, " We tie knots and bind up words in double meanings, and then try to untie them." [32]

With the advent of general semantics, however, the circle has been closed. Each of the separate, though related, dimensions of meaning has claimed exclusive right to the use of the word " semantics." General semantics has claimed the " adequacy " side of the triangle, philosophical semantics has claimed the " truth " side, and linguistic semantics has staked its claim on the " symbolizing " side; clarity has hardly achieved a victory in this struggle.

C. Language as Functional Vocabulary

The several meanings attaching to " semantics " do not make this term unique in the expanded vocabulary of the English language with which we carry on serious conversation and inquiry. This plurality of meaning illustrates a common difficulty that is becoming more evident as an increasing variety of scholars and specialists give their attention to language. It is all but impossible to extract a term from the matrix of concepts with which various special disciplines work. Indeed, it is quite pointless to give an intensional definition of a term so pivotal to three separate but related special fields of inquiry. An extensional or operational definition of "semantics," for example, would of necessity involve the person who asked for it in each of the disciplines for which the term is a peculiar one. For this reason, it becomes clear that technical or special vocabularies, so essential to the pursuit of knowledge, shut off scholars and scientists from one another; these vocabularies also shut off the specialists as a group from the general public for whose benefit, ostensibly, this knowledge is pursued.

Scholars for whom language has become so important a problem as it has in our era have recognized that it is necessary to cross some of the barriers separating one inquiry from another and to attempt some generalizations as to the fundamental outlook enshrined in the various sciences. This is part, at least, of the goal envisaged by logical analysis as a discipline, but the process is thwarted by the rather narrow limits within which the enterprise is viewed. What is called for at this point seems to be a new look at the vocabularies employed by various cultural pursuits. Such a review would lead to a functional or operational aspect of semantics as applied to particular vocabulary complexes within separate tongues.

Before the functional aspect of semantics can be developed, however, certain preliminary problems must be noted. The most important of these problems is that of defining the segment of language upon which such an analysis is to be made. According to the Saussurean model of linguistic science, it is fairly simple to distinguish between two segments of language. For de Saussure, language consisted of several tongues. He employed the French word *le langage* for "human speech-activity in its most general aspects." [33] This is the broad general category of human language which will concern the panchronistic linguist of the future. *Le langage*, in turn, consists of many different instances of *la langue* (tongue); the literal translation of the latter, "tongue," is a fairly common if somewhat obsolescent designation for "a system of symbol-engrams stored in the minds of members of the speech community." [34]

The next subordinate division of *le langage* de Saussure called *la parole* (word). Between *la langue* and *la parole* there is, however, a division of any tongue that consists of the functional vocabulary employed by a segment of the users of that tongue. The boundaries of this segment of a tongue will vary from group to group and even from person to person within such groups. Regardless of the difficulty involved in designating the boundaries of this nebulous segment of *la langue*, the segment must be studied as a decisive factor in any comprehension of the inner semantic structure of a given tongue. Very few speakers of a highly developed tongue have at their immediate command the entire vocabulary of that tongue. The general limits of a speaker's vocabulary actually define the way in which that person, or the group he represents, understands reality.

What has been infrequently recognized by linguistic scientists is that the special vocabulary employed by a designated group of speakers of a particular tongue is more than merely a selection of the words and phrases belonging to that tongue, although, to be sure, it is at least that. The "more" is to be appreciated from, even if it cannot actually be described by, the fact that users of a specialized vocabulary are frequently more able to communicate with speakers of another tongue than they are with speakers of the same tongue who are not accustomed to their peculiar vocabulary. This community of intercourse, or communication, that is possible between one tongue and another seems to suggest that there is something peculiar about the relationship existing among the words and phrases that make up a special vocabulary. It is this sort of observation that prompted Anatol Rapoport to ask "at what point a difference in 'vocabularies' amounts to a difference in 'language.'" [35] The difficulty in dealing with these somewhat indeterminate quantities known as vocabularies is only underlined by this sort of question.

It is at least worth notice, in addition, that while linguistic science has experimented with one classification of tongues into morphologic types, and has made further great strides in classifying tongues into families on the basis of phonemic-lexical similarities, practically no work has been done on a classification system whose basis would be content analysis. The only area of linguistic science in which any work of this sort has been done is that closely related to cultural anthropology. General semantics has made some inroads into this problem, but the type of competence in linguistic science required for this sort of analysis makes it difficult for a general semanticist to do the fundamental research necessary to develop data and evolve theory in such an inquiry. A possibility for advance along this line, that is content analysis applied to vocabularies within tongues, is offered by the Sapir-Whorf hypothesis.

Edward Sapir was an American linguist and cultural anthropologist whose interests lay in the study of the American Indian languages and cultures. Benjamin Whorf's interests paralleled those of Sapir, and both men contributed heavily to linguistic science by their analyses of various American Indian tongues and families of tongues. The Sapir-Whorf hypothesis, stated briefly, is that a language (*langue*) is the index of the manner in which its speakers organize, through the structural semantic system of that tongue, their experience of the world in which they live.[36] The hypothesis was based upon the intimate study of language as a function of the culture in the context of several quite unrelated American Indian cultures. As Harry Hoijer has pointed out, the hypothesis is not strictly a novelty, for its roots are to be found in Herder, Cassirer, Langer, and many others who have been interested in discerning a pattern of language.[37] To these two men belongs, however, the credit for having stated the theory so clearly in the context of the scientific study of language. The hypothesis suggests a strong likelihood that the structural semantic pattern of vocabulary groupings within various tongues may be located somewhat precisely.

The problem of isolating these vocabularies need not present an insurmountable obstacle if they are viewed in their proper contexts. To all intents and purposes, the vocabulary peculiar to a specific group of speakers is already singled out in the literature that comprises their findings and their conversations. Instead, however, of seeking some previously prepared lexicon of the tongue in which the special vocabulary exists, it would be scientifically more fruitful to describe the vocabulary in terms of the way in which it operates. A functional vocabulary, such as that which, for example, a nuclear physicist employs, is a structural semantic system for organizing and communicating a particular variety of experience which, in his case, is derived from laboratory experiment. Thus his vocabulary is a calculus of terms taken from his native tongue the locus of whose meaning is to be found in the relation of these terms to one another. The meaning of any term within this calculus depends entirely upon the nature of the experience reported and the relationships among the terms employed to organize the complex of experience and generalize about it. Just as the Indian languages studied by Sapir and Whorf, these functional vocabularies are an index to the metalinguistic patterns that are operative within the structural semantic systems employed by the users of these vocabularies. Likewise, as several tongues exhibit a common origin and frequently share much of the same store of " symbol-engrams," so these functional vocabularies exhibit a phonemic-lexical affinity with one another but are in every sense independent tongues within tongues. Their functional semantic relation to similar vocabularies in other tongues can be paralleled by the morphological similarity between Chinese and English, which are from the phonemic-lexical viewpoint entirely unrelated. The semantic relation between the " language of physics " in German and the " language of physics" in Russian happens to be considerably greater, however, than the morphological relation between Chinese and English.

Although these separate functional vocabularies have existed for a considerable period of time within the tongues whose speakers have been more active in a scientific and inquiring way, the problem of communication among highly specialized lines of inquiry has tended to point up the fact and bring it into closer focus as a legitimate subject for semantic study. While empirical studies such as the natural sciences, and to a somewhat lesser degree the social sciences, were in the process of developing special vocabularies, these sciences were also developing a peculiar semantic structure that resulted from the kinds of experience with which they were preoccupied. This observation is confirmed by the rather clear declarations of logical empiricism as to the kinds of statements the natural scientist considers as meaningful. The discomfort experienced by the philosophers of symbolic form and the philosophers of existence with this narrowing of the possible area of meaningful discourse strongly suggests that they operate within a different type of semantic structure despite the fact that many of them speak the same tongue as the logical empiricist. Thus it would seem that a *tongue* consists of several functional vocabularies each of which exhibits its own semantic structure. This semantic structure is due to the way in which the community of speakers, to whom the functional vocabulary is common, organize and structure experience.

Because special interest groups and special fields of inquiry develop vocabularies by invention or by isolating words in the common store and assigning them specific meanings, each of them has a store of terms which are very nearly univocal within the defined group of speakers. The specialized uses of terms frequently find their way into unabridged dictionaries and, of course, are to be found in the numerous handbooks compiled for guidance in studying the technical literature of the sciences or other disciplines.

Although it is possible to compile dictionaries of various scientific vocabularies, this enterprise breaks down as soon as we leave the domain of the primarily denotative type of language. The sciences and many of the more humanistic disciplines operate with a largely denotative vocabulary, and this is frequently a source of misunderstanding when it comes to appreciating the semantic structure of scientific thought. On the other hand, the literature, in the classical sense, which a culture produces and which reflects the dynamic of culture, is written in a largely connotative language. For this reason, it is frequently difficult to find compilations of metaphor and other expressive devices employed by poets and prose writers. In order to appreciate this vocabulary and to sample its structural semantic, it is necessary to go to the literature itself. An important use of this sort of language is to be found in the religious literature of the ages.

Like poetry, religious literature means to be more than informative, more than expository. Its aim is to share experience and the insights that come from experience. The free use of image and metaphor, so common to religious literature, invites the one addressed into dialogue not only at the intellectual level but at the deeper levels at the same time. The orderly and systematic exposition of a thesis by a scientist or a logician frequently makes of the hearer an object — information *about* something is being *imparted* to another. The orator or the preacher, the poet or the prophet, each demands more than the presence of an audience, and each aims at more than even the loftiest instruction of his hearers. The vocabulary employed is as much a "technical vocabulary" as understood, heretofore, as any of the scientific vocabularies. It is also a vocabulary each of whose component parts acquires its meaning from the total context in which the terms are used.

The "technical" quality of the vocabulary of religious affirmation can be illustrated by referring to the baptismal symbol known as the Apostles' Creed. Anyone, Christian or otherwise, who reads or hears this creed cannot but grant the stark simplicity of its vocabulary. He may recoil at what it says, shrieking, "Absurd!" He cannot call it either complex or abstruse. Further, the scope of its reference is astounding, and this scope of reference is accomplished by way of, rather than in spite of, its simple vocabulary. This confession of faith is cast against the "all and more" that is contained in the overworked word "universe," and it testifies to a concern for totality as well as the minutest detail, for the remotest past as well as the most distant future. Yet for all that reach into and beyond space and time, the merely consecutive, it preserves the uniqueness and singularity of concrete person in equally concrete event — the Jesus of history is at once the Lord of history. Finally, what holds it together is the pervasive context of commitment. This simplicity, this universal scope, and this personal concrete history all become the concern as well as the history of the " I " who, by this affirmation, is incorporated into the " we " whose history and concern it has been and continues to be.

The vocabulary of religious affirmation, as exhibited in the Apostles' Creed, differs from the vocabulary of the descriptive sciences in that it is concrete, personal, historical, and evocative. The combination of successive phrases looks propositional and discursive, but it is far better described by the term " presentational," which we have already used in connection with the philosophy of symbolic form. The frame of reference in which the creed is to be seen and from which it is to be understood is a liturgical framework. As the summary statement of a much more elaborate historical continuum contained in the Bible of the Christian church, the creed is more like psalms, hymns, prayers, and blessings — the sort of utterance which makes up so much of the language in which the Christian church *speaks* when it is at worship. In the truest sense, the Apostles' Creed is esoteric rather than exoteric; it is not uttered from the detached viewpoint of an observer but from the committed viewpoint of a participant. Although psalms, hymns, or prayers are usually cast in the second person, addressed to God as participant in the dialogue with his people, the creeds have a deceptive quality of speaking *about* rather than *to* God. It appears as though the creeds are spoken from the viewpoint of the observer. This is simply for the reason that within the context from which it is uttered, the third person references to God the Father, to Jesus the Christ, and to the Holy Spirit are references to the unique God known in the experience of the community called the church. These apparently third person references are shared among those who know the unique God first of all as the Thou of liturgical language. As the Bible is not addressed to the "world" but to the church, so is the Apostles' Creed directed to the church; both are directed, also, from the church to the unique God whose activity is discerned in the specific historical framework related therein. This vocabulary, then, can be penetrated only by participation in the life of that community. For this reason, we must call it *religious* language, the vehicle of commitment.

Midway between the poles created by the scientific vocabulary on one side and the religious vocabulary on the other stands the language of the theologian. The peculiar mission of the theologian makes it necessary for him to be amphibious. He is engaged in the two-way conversation of interpreting the church to the "world" and the "world" to the church. As the etymology of the word suggests, theology is that branch of inquiry which gives a reasonable exposition (*logos* is Greek for "reason") of a belief in God (*theos* is Greek for "god"). Christian theology is specifically concerned with giving a reasonable account of the precisely Christian belief in God. The language of prayer, i.e., religious language, expresses the unity and distinction in God as an address, "through Jesus Christ our Lord, who with thee and the Holy Ghost liveth and reigneth ever, one God, world without end." [38] The language of theology makes the same affirmation in a propositional form, e.g., "In one God there are three persons." This latter statement is an inference drawn by the reasoning process from the empirical evidence of the life history of the Christian church, beginning from the awareness among the Israelite people of the uniqueness of their history and extending through the historical life of Jesus out into the life of that community which flows from him as its center. Theology is not an exclusively empirical science, however, for it is chiefly involved in historical facts rather than with data of sense observation. It should be designated as a historical science, for it generalizes from a specific historical continuum. Its primary occupation is to expound what that specific continuum of history means and implies.

The distinction drawn between religious and theological language on the basis of function will not automatically eliminate all problems of Christian communication. As a modest proposal, however, it should obviate some of the more sweeping objections to the validity of either type of language. From the viewpoint of function, the vocabulary of theology is roughly parallel to the vocabulary of the descriptive sciences; as a historical science, theology performs a service similar to that performed by the natural and social sciences. That is to say, theology sets forth and organizes a selected set of empirical observations. It matters but little in this connection that the natural and social sciences expound a given realm of natural and social phenomena and theology a specific grouping of historical phenomena.

From the descriptive viewpoint, the vocabulary employed by the historical sciences is determined quite as much by the method of history as the vocabulary of natural science is determined by the scientific method. This observation implies that each of these vocabularies has its own peculiar semantic structure. As a method, however, the canons of scientific observation and generalization have been codified but recently; this is particularly evident when we survey the panorama of European thought from the pre-Socratics to Whitehead. Historical method is still in its infancy when compared to the inductive method of science which has accounted for the phenomenal development of scientific inquiry in the past hundred years. Consequently, if we are to understand in what way the vocabulary and semantic structure of theological language is meaningful and useful for communication, we shall have to look closely at the context in which theology operates as a science. That is to say, we shall have to view the theological vocabulary as a structural semantic system within which there is operative a specific way of organizing and previsioning experience.

Chapter IV

Language, Myth, and Logic

The tentative distinctions among vocabularies peculiar to various spheres of interest drawn at the close of the preceding chapter were an attempt to set the stage for a semantic consideration of a particular variety of vocabulary. It was obvious that by "vocabulary" something more than mere words was implied. The complexes into which words enter, syntactic units such as phrases and clauses, modify the meaning of the words themselves; in fact, the meaning of any word is a function of its use, and it is only false abstraction that considers a word to have a meaning independent of its use in syntactic units. We have preferred "vocabulary" in order that we might avoid the confusion that results from the ambiguity of the word "language." Our purpose in this chapter will be to test the hypothesis that the vocabulary of theological discourse is analyzable from the viewpoint of its internal semantic structure.

Linguistic semanticists have contributed heavily to a method whereby the total vocabulary of a given language can be analyzed from both the descriptive and historical perspectives. If their method is valid in connection with the total vocabulary of a given tongue, we have some precedent upon which to operate in applying the method to a specialized vocabulary that constitutes something of a "language within a language." The compilers of theological word books, historical lexicons of the Biblical languages, and specialized lexicons of patristic writings have made an exciting venture into the area of lexical semantics. Although these scholars might not have been consciously applying the principles of linguistic science in their efforts, what they have accomplished provides a good supply of raw material out of which the viewpoint of the theological vocabulary may be developed. Less spectacular and infinitely less exciting are the concordances that have been compiled by painstaking scholars of the vernacular versions as well as the original versions of the Bible text. One task that remains to be done is the sorting out of the descriptive and historical dimensions of these various vocabularies. This would bring to full fruition the essay in lexical semantics begun with the first glossaries of Biblical terms.

More decisively needed at this point, however, is the extension of semantic studies in the theological vocabulary to include the level of what we have described as functional semantics. This enterprise will also have its descriptive and historical aspects. Although such an undertaking may seem to encroach upon the domain of the logician, it will seem so only to those who have made the a priori judgment that all language, regardless of its type, applies a universal or natural logic. As Jespersen pointed out more than thirty years ago, hardly anyone would have dreamed of making this sort of judgment regarding the morphology of language [39]; yet beneath much of the discussion involving syntax, one can detect a tendency toward the notion that there is a universal pattern of syntax corresponding to what is, however incorrectly, assumed to be basic in all human speech. Thus, once a linguistic scientist begins to inquire about the meaning of sentence forms and what this can show us about the internal logic of a given tongue, a number of preconceptions arise about how human language and human thought are related to reality. Regardless of such objections, however, the question must be raised. The question at issue is whether or not the logic of expression involved in the religious vocabulary is the same logic as that which is assumed to govern mathematical inference or scientific generalization. [40] Fundamentally, of course, this is a question concerning the logic of a specific variety of mythic expression. The question will also involve the canons for translating that type of expression from the vocabulary in which it is congenial into another which is less than congenial to it. This problem is exhibited, in part at least, in the translation of Biblical literature into some of the languages which are quite foreign to both the Indo-European languages and the Semitic tongues.

It is patently impossible to cover in detail the entire range of the Judaeo-Christian religious vocabulary because there are so many levels existent in the Bible. Each of these levels is itself a complicated network of related notions and categories making up a structural semantic system. Ideally, each level should be described in detail, and no historical conclusions should be made until each of the levels involved in such conclusion has been adequately described. As in the case of lexical semantics, we are not without a good supply of raw material to work upon. There is an abundance of monographic studies in Biblical literature, in liturgiology, and in patristic literature which deal with what are clearly semantic problems. Here, too, the main task is that of sorting out the descriptive materials from the historical conclusions in order to organize the field for study. Instead, therefore, of trying to deal exhaustively with all of the factors at all of the various levels of transmission of the Biblical vocabulary, we shall attempt to carry the discussion forward on thematic lines in the hope that we can discern a direction that this vocabulary takes.

A. The Mythic Stance of the Old Testament

It is a commonplace of modern Biblical study to speak of certain aspects of the Biblical narrative as myth and to characterize the expression in these parts of the Bible as mythic. A recent writer has indicated that one of the typical problems involved in analyzing religious language is that of distinguishing between factual propositions and figurative statements.[41] The process of distinguishing is not complete, however, until some steps have been taken to discover what the mythic statements mean.

As a term used to designate a particular type of narrative and the thinking involved in the production of such narrative, "myth" does not mean the same thing to all who employ the term as scholars. R. G. Collingwood contends that "myth proper has always the character of *theogony*." [42] This notion of myth arises from Collingwood's having used the Babylonian *Poem on Creation* as a type of myth. He does distinguish the Hebrew use of myth on the grounds that "it replaces theogony by ethnogony." [43] If Hebrew myth replaces the story of the origin of the gods by a story of the origin of the nation, it would appear to lack the distinct character of "myth proper"; hence, it is hard to see precisely what Collingwood understands myth to be. In terms almost diametrically opposed to those of Collingwood, Susanne Langer states, "Divinities are born of ritual, but theologies spring from myth." [44] Her distinctions among myth, legend, and fairy tale (*Märchen*) follow those underlying the study of the myths, sagas, and fairy tales which are so abundant in the early history of the Germanic peoples. The chief characteristics of myth, according to this view, are its confrontation of the actual world and its determination to understand and organize experience. That is to say, among those who have studied German saga literature, myth is a means of orientation to the world that actually is, and is not a vehicle for escape from it. This is an important refinement of the definition of myth, since it removes it from the realm of the merely untrue. Yet, even this refinement of what myth does will not satisfactorily account for the distinctive feature of the Hebrew myth — its concern with time and history.

If it be maintained that myth arises only when the relationships of mankind to cosmic forces, that is to nature, "are conceived through the spontaneous metaphor of poetic fantasy," [45] then myth does not designate the peculiar stance of the Biblical literature toward time. In fact, the Biblical myth, which provides the framework in which the entire story of salvation is recounted, is inextricably bound up with a keen awareness of time. No explanation of the cosmic outlook of the Old Testament — and this is equally true of the New Testament — which slights the Hebrew valuation of time and history as basic to that outlook can do any justice to the peculiarly Biblical view of reality. Alan Richardson sums up the Biblical preference for time as a fundamental category when, in the course of pointing out that the Bible is enclosed within two internally related myths, he says, "whereas the one myth affirms: 'In the beginning God,' so the other declares: 'at the end Christ.'" [46]

At the one end of the Biblical narrative we encounter the creation myth, and at the other we are confronted with the myth of the *eschaton,* the end of time. Throughout the entire length of the Bible from Genesis to Revelation, however, these two myths not only recur but actually provide the locus of the story which orients man in the world. It is profoundly significant that neither the religion of the Old Testament nor that of the New is at all concerned with what happened *before* "the beginning" or what happens *after* "the end." The Christian proclamation somewhat alters the perspective by designating Jesus as the Christ or the bringer of "the end," but the end that God brings into history in Jesus the Christ is a foretaste of the real end toward which time and history move. Only the reintroduction of the dualistic world outlook, which the Hebrew-Christian myth excluded, has been able to turn the Christian proclamation into a promise of escape and extrication to some far-off paradise.

The process by which the book of Genesis achieved its present form testifies to the primary concern for history of the community for whom this book was the first chapter of its sacred history. The earliest account, forming the basis upon which all later expansions were made, consisted largely of *legends;* the primary stratum of the book of Genesis is a series of *legends.* A legend contains a kernel of historical fact inside a story that is elaborated in the retelling and expanded until it reaches the proportions of a narrative of the size and complexity of the Abraham story or the Joseph story. The compiler of the earliest narrative in Genesis meant to relate a series of legends of diverse origins one to another in order that the legends belonging to various groups in the Israelite amphictyony might be brought into a coherent whole. His purpose was that of relating the pastoral tradition of the desert tribes to the indigenous Palestinian tradition so that the whole could serve as a continuous religious tradition for a people lately unified into one nation. At this stage of the Genesis tradition, the mythic element is practically nil. It was not until the first significant revision of this catena of legends that myth made its appearance in the tradition of Israel as a vehicle for expression.

Of the two Creation stories in Genesis (Gen. 1:1 to 2:4a; 2:4b-25), the J story (Gen. 2:4b-25) is clearly the older. This older narrative itself consists of two definitely discernible strata that have been fused into a single unit. As Dr. Simpson has adequately maintained,[47] the final form of this earlier narrative contained some distinctly modified version of the Babylonian creation myth as it was known to the Canaanites. In its original Babylonian or even its Canaanite context, this myth would qualify for Collingwood's characterization of myth; that is to say, it is not only theogonic, but it is cosmogonic as well — it relates the *origin* of the gods and of the world. In that context, however, the myth is not historical, nor does it relate necessarily to a concrete group of people or nation. The Israelite writer responsible for the developed version of the earlier stratum of the Genesis narrative used as much of the myth as he could profitably employ. His purpose was to show, by modification of the thrust of the myth, that the God of Israel, Yahweh, whom the Israelites had come to know in such concrete historical events as are related in the Song of Deborah (Judg., ch. 5) or in the Song of Miriam (Ex. 15:21) was not only more than a tribal deity — he was the foundation of the world that is. The manner in which he accomplished this purpose was to expand backward the catena of legend which preserved a series of encounters with Yahweh — Abraham, Jacob, Joseph, etc. When the considerably modified form of the creation myth was prefaced to this expanded account, it served to identify the Yahweh of historical encounter as the creator and sustainer of the world. This order of identification is of vital importance to an understanding of the peculiarly Israelite use of myth, for it indicates most clearly that the earliest category of Israelite theological reflection was *history* and *not nature*. Corroboration of this viewpoint is supplied by the fact that the normal designation of Yahweh is " the God of your fathers, the God of Abraham, the God of Isaac, and the God of Jacob " (Ex. 3:15 f.; 4:5; cf. chs. 2:24; 6:3, 8; 32:13; 33:1; Num. 32:11; Deut. 1:8; 6:10; 9:5, 27, etc.). Except for certain oblique references in the latter sections of the Second Isaiah, God is not designated as the creator until the apocryphal Book of Jubilees.

The final redaction of the Israelite sacred history as it is presented in the Pentateuch was accomplished by the Priestly writer. Although his hand is visible throughout the story from Genesis through Joshua, one of the most significant achievements of this writer is his revision of the Creation story. The Creation story which now opens the book of Genesis (Gen. 1:1 to 2:4a) is his restatement of the Babylonian myth purged of those cosmogonic remnants which the earlier writer had felt it necessary to retain in his own modification of that myth. The peculiarly Israelite orientation of the Priestly writer is evident from his concern for the primarily historical character of the act of creation. His interest in the historical depth of this act, cosmogonically conceived in his source, comes through in unmistakable outline, for this account contains the seeds of a doctrine of *creatio ex nihilo*, even if it does not articulately express such a doctrine.[48] It must not be construed, however, that the doctrine of *creatio ex nihilo* is a metaphysical generalization made by the Priestly writer.

In this mythic conception, as presented in Genesis, we encounter an instance par excellence of the distinction between mythic expression and philosophical speculation. If God's creative act was performed upon an already existent matter, then from the historical viewpoint, God is not ultimate; there is a basically dualistic foundation to the universe if this view is carried to its logical conclusion. Depending upon the way in which the first two Hebrew words are translated at the beginning of Genesis, one can arrive at either a monistic or dualistic conception of the ultimate character of the Israelite view of reality.

The mythic vehicle employed by the Priestly writer is not primarily concerned with cosmogony, however, but it is a religious affirmation cast against what, to him, is an inadequate conception of ultimate reality — the Babylonian creation myth. Apparently, nothing was conceivable for him before the beginning of God's creative activity; hence, his view comes from the inside of the historical process which he projects backward. The metaphysical view would be an *exterior* view in which the narrator would be attempting to achieve an objective detachment, a platform from which he could view the process. He, like his fellow Israelites, construed God as active and historical rather than quiescent and atemporal. Consequently, the beginning of the creative process is the only point to which it is possible to attain, and anything behind this point would have to speak of a quiescent and atemporal God, a notion that is simply inconceivable to an Israelite. Because of the historical orientation of the community represented by the Priestly writer, he was under pressure to change the naturalistic orientation of the source myth so that it would reflect the primacy of history over nature as the fundamental category of Israelite conception of God and the world. The measure of his achievement is stamped over the entire structure of the Pentateuch, and it carries forward into the Former Prophets reaching a type of conclusion in the Priestly version of history contained in the works of the Chronicler and Ezra-Nehemiah.

The nature myth was persistent in the milieu in which Israel hammered out its conception of Yahweh, the God who acts. The hardiness of this mythic conception is demonstrated by the prophetic literature. While the incipient theological viewpoint of the Pentateuch was taking shape as a challenge to the generalized Semitic myth of creation, the prophets were waging war in the name of Yahweh against the fertility ceremonials which are characterized by the name Baalism. The cultic observances of Baalism were a response to the Canaanite manifestation of that variety of myth which arises among a settled agricultural people. In some form or other, this myth of the regularity of the seasons of planting, growing, and harvesting appeared among all the ancient people of the Mediterranean and the Near East. The myths of Demeter, Ceres, Syra Dea, and even Isis and Osiris are all localized forms of mythic generalization based upon the cyclic occurrence of the seasons as well as the precarious plight of the man who depends for sustenance upon the whims of the seasonal rains. In another form, this mythic outlook rises among a people whose lives depend upon viticulture. The Dionysiac rites are related to this cycle of myth.

The consolidation of the Israelite community brought into close proximity tribes of people who had varied backgrounds. On the one hand, there were those whose lives had been bound up in the agricultural processes of Canaan. They were the settled peoples against whom the invasion by pastoral and nomadic tribes had been mounted. Their outlook was essentially a cyclic one, for they knew the endless round of seasons and the difficulties of extracting a living out of the land. Their entire mythic structure was based upon this experience. On the other hand, the pastoral and nomadic tribes who had come into the land and taken control by force were differently oriented. The precariousness of existence on the desert wastes where there was little grazing for the flocks emphasized the transitoriness of life. Being nomadic, they could not appreciate the meaning of settled existence, nor could they have had that kind of experience which speaks of regularity. Tomorrow and another grazing land were their hope; hence, time and history were the ingredients of their mythic structure.

The fundamental insight of the prophets was the recognition of the primacy of history for the life of the world as well as for its beginning. Therefore, from the days of Elijah onward, the prophets continued to inveigh strongly against the tendency to turn the Yahweh of historical encounter into an image, however exalted, of the gods of nature and the natural processes. The stock in trade of the prophets as they made their declarations was the destructive power of Yahweh, whose sovereignty tolerated no manipulation by mimetic cult. The message of the prophets had two dimensions that were really but two aspects of the same dimension. Their twin targets were settled agricultural existence and settled political existence. These targets were represented by Baalism and the monarchy, both of which were manifestations of their having deserted the religion of the fathers.

The establishment of the monarchy in Israel meant that the nation had made certain concessions to settled political existence. The corollaries of this act of concession were to be found in the shifting alliances made by the Israelite nation in order both to preserve its identity and to engage in political activity in the seething Middle East. Despite the fact that there were gains in Israel's national status, its achievement signified than an idol had replaced Yahweh, for security became more important than service to God who had chosen this people for his own. The development of agriculture and viticulture was, on its own level, a manifestation of the same idolatry, for Baal replaced Yahweh. So bitter was the opposition to this agricultural religion that the festivals that belonged to its observance were radically transformed in the prophetic period. The two early festivals of Passover and Pentecost were agricultural in origin and represented the offering of the early harvests. The

Old Testament witnesses to their transformation into feasts of
a historical genre having to do with the *wandering* period of
Israelite life.

Passover was related to the exodus and Pentecost to the
giving of the law at Sinai; thus, even at the level of observance
there was reflected a radical abhorrence of the generalized
Semitic myth of the cyclic return of the seasons. Less successful was the transformation of the feast that related to viticulture, the Feast of Tabernacles. Nevertheless, there are clear
indications that this feast was reoriented by likening the living
in temporary dwellings, required once the grape harvest starts,
to the wandering in the wilderness for forty years. The super-
ficialities of this transformation were recognizable, since the
more orgiastic features of the old grape festival were transferred to the temple court in the form of dances and other observances. The process continued even into the second century
B.C. when the feast of the winter solstice, Chanukah, was invested with rites, ceremonies, and meaning, linking it to the
victory of Judas Maccabaeus over Antiochus Epiphanes (167
B.C.).

Against these twin manifestations of trading precariousness
for security, the monarchy and Baalism, the prophets declared
the wrath of Yahweh. The orientation toward nature reflected
both in Baalism and in dependence upon the monarchy dramatized the serenity and passivity of God, but the prophetic
orientation toward the emergent nature of history made the
judgment of God a prime category. Baalism looked toward
predictability, but the prophets demanded response. In the
face of the cult of action, the prophets seemed to say:

> If you would understand the character of Yahweh, the God
> of Israel, look not to the orderly pattern of day upon day,
> season upon season. The God of Israel has brought all that
> into being by his word, and he can put an end to it by his
> word. Hear the Word of Yahweh (the God of Abraham, of
> Isaac, and of Jacob): "You only have I known! See that I
> have chosen you in the nexus of historical event, and in those

same events I can reject you." If you would learn what is
your origin and destiny, what Yahweh requires of you, look
what he has done for your fathers; then return to him in
trust and faithfulness. He will forgive your rejection of him.
But if you turn not, he can and will destroy — he will bring
this whole round of regularity and endless cycle to an end
tumbling about your ears.

Here, then, in the prophetic strain is also a sharp challenge
to the primacy of nature as a category for understanding the
ultimate meaning of the world and existence. The structure
against which the theologians of the Pentateuch as well as the
prophets struggled   together was a mythic generalization of
the natural processes as those generalizations had been made
by Babylonian cosmogonists or Canaanite naturalists. Against
the universalistic thinking of the Babylonian or the Canaanite,
the Israelite Yahwists posed singularity — the category of a particular history as the key to an adequate understanding of the
world as they experienced it.

The logical outcome of prophecy was apocalyptic. As the
Pentateuchal writers reflected upon the historical meaning of
creation, so the successors of the prophets worked out the
historical meaning of finality. The infiltration of the eschatological myth, whose origin is to be sought in the same general
region as that which produced the creation myth, follows a
pattern similar to that which explains the Israelite use of the
creation myth. As the Israelite community's successor Judaism
developed the myth of the end, there was no longer a unified
political entity with ecclesiastical jurisdiction. Hence, there
are but hints in the Hebrew canon of a developed eschatology.

The only book in the Old Testament that contains anything
approaching a systematic eschatology is The Book of Daniel;
even here the rough outlines hardly suffice for a systematic
discussion or presentation of the myth of the end in a way
comparable to the creation myth. In its present form, The Book
of Daniel reflects the last period during which Israel had independent hegemony. It is interesting to speculate upon what

the eschatology might have looked like had it been permitted to take shape in a milieu similar to that in which the doctrine of creation reached fruition. The history of the last century or so of Roman domination of Israel's remnant successor prevents one from delving too deeply into this question, but one conclusion does seem inevitable. Just as the doctrine of creation was not arrived at by generalization from the observed regularity of natural processes, so the eschatology of Judaism was not derived from any observed devolution of natural processes. As a matter of fact, the origin of eschatology in the prophetic period took place in a milieu in which Israel enjoyed great prosperity. Both creation and the *eschaton* are historical categories and must be seen historically. The way in which this eschatology did develop can be seen by observing the mythic framework in which the person of Jesus was evaluated by the Jews in whose midst he appeared.

B. The Mythic Stance of the Christian Gospel

The magnitude of the debate engendered by the brief essay written by Rudolf Bultmann less than twenty years ago leads one who is not at all expert in theological argument to suspect that there is something to the view that the New Testament is cast in mythic forms. His suspicion becomes more like a definite conviction, pro or con, when he reads the several possible definitions of myth. As we have developed the category of myth in the Old Testament, it is quite apparent that we are dealing with the very stuff out of which the Christian message is forged. If this stuff is excised or reduced to some other "stuff," the essential thrust of the gospel loses its uniqueness and is hardly distinguishable from any system of ethics or religion. Before we discuss the problem of how this translation is to be accomplished, we must look more closely at the Christian myth itself. Here we shall realize that to excise the myth would be similar to taking the warp out of a fabric — removal of the warp produces a pile of string which is no longer a fabric.

We have already referred to the Apostles' Creed as a suffi-
cient summary of the Christian proclamation. A further analysis of this affirmation that is made by the newly baptized
Christian will reveal enough of the mythic quality of the Christian gospel to indicate the depth to which it penetrates the
fabric of the message. We shall examine the various statements
of this creed, but our attention will be focused upon those
which illuminate the mythic structure of the proclamation.
This process will expose the mythic stance of the gospel.

In the first place, of course, it will be recognized that we
have already examined what is implied in the first few words
of the creed: (I believe in) *God the Father Almighty, Maker
of heaven and earth.* This was, in large measure, the intention
in the preceding section of this chapter. The addition of this
phrase to the creed in its present form dates from a period
when the baptizands were those who had not shared the
Israelite faith and orientation previously. As a product of the
Gentile Christian church, its presence in the creed is actually
an affirmation that the church intended to be construed as
legitimate successor to the Israelite community and that it
shared faith in the God of history to which the literature of that
community was a witness. We have also touched upon an important aspect of a phrase that appears later in the creed: *he*
(Jesus) *shall come to judge the quick and the dead.* This phrase
embodies that eschatology which is a tenet of orthodox Judaism, although its precise formulation here would not be at all
acceptable to an orthodox Jew. The specific alteration to
orthodox eschatology made by this affirmation will be discussed under the last article of the creed.

The second paragraph of the creed resembles, in its general
outline and thrust, what has been called the *kērygma* [49] of the
early church. Since *kērygma*, in Greek, means "what is proclaimed," we can see that the early Christian proclamation
bears marked resemblance to what the church required its
constituents to affirm about the person of Jesus who was the
focal point of the Christian affirmation; thus we are justified

in looking to this affirmation for the structure of early Christian belief. More than their being merely summaries of the New Testament faith, these affirmations also presuppose the mythic context of the Old Testament and the community for whom it was Scripture; in other words, the Hebrew Bible was also the Bible of the Christians. The continuity between the two communities, Israel and the church, is reflected in the irrefragable bond between the Old and New Testaments in the church. One of the clearest indications of this bond is provided in the opening phrase of the second paragraph of the creed which we now bring more closely into focus.

And in Jesus Christ his only Son our Lord. The designation of Jesus as *his only Son* immediately forces us back to the first clause in order to find the antecedent of the possessive pronoun "his." There we discover that Jesus is God's (*Yahweh's*) only son, but we may not stop there. The Old Testament doctrine of God in its entirety is contained in the summary descriptions "Father Almighty" and "Maker of heaven and earth." The only way in which this affirmation understands God, then, is in terms of the historical and mythic presentation of the Old Testament. One of the earliest difficulties that beset the Christian church was created by the choice of the somewhat colorless Greek word *theos* to render both of the richer and more expressive terms of the Hebrew.

The more distinctive name of the God of Israel, Yahweh (Ex. 3:14), is the abstract noun formed from the Hebrew verb frequently, if erroneously, translated "to be"; or else, it is the third person singular imperfect of that same verb.[50] In either case, it is a form that soon became a proper noun. In the nearly seven thousand occurrences of it in the Masoretic text of the Old Testatment, it is pointed to be read *adonai* which, when translated, means "lord, master" in English. This feature of the Hebrew locution accounts for the prevalence of the words *dominus* in Latin and *kyrios* in Greek as designations for the God of Israel. The less frequent name for God in the Old Testament is elohim, a plural of the generic name for deity, and it corresponds to the words " god " in English, *deus* in Latin, and *theos* in Greek. In its Hebrew form, it is what is known as a plural of majesty, and it is used to indicate that the God of Israel is the epitome of all the characteristics attributed to the many lesser gods. In English, the convention adopted is the use of the capital initial to achieve the same effect. Nevertheless, the use of this name for God in the creed assures that the mythic framework of the Old Testament will be preserved.

Against this background, the historical figure known as Jesus of Nazareth has been evaluated and described; that is to say, Jesus is identified within a mythic structure and his significance is expounded in terms of that structure. He is a definite historical individual, who was born and died, but whose life has been set forth in terms of the Old Testament myth of the God who was encountered in historical event, Yahweh. The process by which the identification was made has much similarity to the process by which Yahweh, the God encountered in history, was identified as the creator and the one who can and will bring the temporal scheme to an abrupt end. The specific degree of relationship posited between the God of Israel and Jesus of Nazareth is that of father and son, but the obvious logic of this assertion, when it is treated as a discursive proposition, renders it meaningless. The logic of the myth is not, however, the grammatical logic of types and predication; the logic with which we are dealing here arises from the peculiar character of the utterance. There is no intention to make a biological assertion here; that is obvious. This is an evaluative utterance and not a proposition about the origin of Jesus. This becomes clearer as we proceed.

Who was conceived by the Holy Ghost, born of the Virgin Mary. At once the structural semantic of the myth becomes much clearer in the circumstances reported of the origin of Jesus. *That* he was born is as historical a statement as those which follow: *suffered under* (during the time of) *Pontius Pilate, was crucified, dead, and buried.* The apparently miraculous character of the birth of Jesus is another sort of statement

altogether. This language belongs with the previous phrase,
"his only Son." It is not of the character of legend, for it really
purports to speak of valuation of the human being Jesus of
Nazareth. The only part of this statement which partakes of
the legendary is the identification of his mother — this does
have a kernel of the historical about it, for she is not further
identified. Whether this aspect, the miraculous birth of Jesus,
which is so much a part of the mythic structure, arose through
application to Jesus of the prophecy of Isaiah delivered to
Ahaz, the king of Judah (Isa. 7:14), as would appear from
Matthew's infancy story (Matt. 2:23), or came about through
the application to Jesus of a type of miraculous birth such as
that of Isaac (Gen. 18: 10-15; 21:1-5) or of Samuel (I Sam.
1:11-20) is not easy to determine. At least one and perhaps
both of these images lie behind this evaluative assertion made
in the form of a historical statement. The significance of the
virgin birth is quite clear, however, in the mythic context in
which Jesus is identified as the Son of God. At its appearance
in this mythical context, the virgin birth belongs to the same
class of assertion as that which appears in the Prologue to the
Fourth Gospel (John 1:1-18), where Jesus is made participant
in the very creative act of God — as pre-existent Logos, Jesus
is there made the *agent* of creation.

Such statements assert the uniqueness of Jesus not in terms
of his moral excellence nor of his thaumaturgic superiority but
in terms of an act of God who is known and encountered in
history. Each of these statements is another way of coming to
terms with the primacy of history as the arena of Yahweh's
activity because he is the Lord of history, both of its beginning
and of its end. The virgin birth of Jesus as an instance, even
the only instance, of parthenogenesis is not of the order of history but of the order of nature; as a datum of nature it would
be patient of several explanations, but as an affirmation of the
act of Yahweh, it is a mythic assertion that finds its meaning in
the life, death, and abiding significance of Jesus, who as the
Christ is the eschatological act of the God of Israel. To put it

more succinctly, the virgin birth of Jesus is not an assertion
about the physical status of a Hebrew maiden but an affirmation about the relation of Jesus to the God of Israel. Some
deeper apprehension of this distinction might have saved the
Christian church centuries of misunderstanding both inside
and outside the community.

*The third day he rose again from the dead (he ascended
into heaven and sitteth on the right hand of God the Father
Almighty).* Two real difficulties are concealed beneath the first
clause: one of them has to do with the verb and the other with
the phrase "from the dead." In the earliest discussion of the
resurrection of Jesus in the New Testament (I Cor., ch. 15),
it is quite clear from the Greek text of Paul's argument that
he is using the same mythic structure as that which pervades
the Old Testament and which is also quite evidently the framework of the preaching of Jesus. Paul's way of characterizing
the resurrection is not that it is an act of Jesus; Paul does not
say that Jesus *rose* (arose) from the dead, but that he *was
raised.* Consequently, it is not quite correct to say that Jesus
is the *risen* Lord but rather that he is the *raised* Lord. This
way of putting the statement indicates that Jesus himself was
not the motive force in this act; he is rather the act of God.
The passive voice, which Paul uses, hides a subject as actor,
and that subject is God. At a very early point in the transmission of the Christian tradition a subtle change in the voice of
the verb appears to have been made. The earliest recensions of
the Apostles' Creed in Greek or in Latin all stem from a time
after this alteration had been made. Thus, there is a break between the New Testament understanding of the way in which
Jesus overcame death, at least in Paul's terms, and the way in
which the creed states it.

The slight shift in thrust of the verb *raise* is understandable
from two viewpoints. One of them is linguistic and the other
stems from the religious attitude of the church. In Hebrew,
there is really no way of distinguishing between a passive form
of a transitive verb and the corresponding intransitive form of

a closely related verb. "To rise" means either to have been raised or to have raised oneself. This subtle distinction could not be preserved in the Greek without serious attention to the use of the middle voice. The gradual shift from the verb *egeirō* (raise) to the verb *anistēmi* (raise, rise) blurred any possible distinction so that Jesus could become the subject of the verb indicating his rising.

As the church developed its theology, there is an increasingly miraculous character attributed to Jesus as the Christ. His human characteristics fade into the background as his thaumaturgic and clairvoyant qualities assume a larger role. In part, this development may be due to a decreasing appreciation of the peculiar structure of the Biblical myth, but in part it is also due to the burgeoning piety of a chiefly liturgical church. Together, this increasing piety and the blurred distinction in the verb forms co-operate to confuse the Hellenistic Christian picture of the peculiar role played by Jesus in the drama of the acts of God. The result of this confusion is a heavier concentration of attention upon the *nature* of Jesus as the Christ with a decreasing concern for the centrality of God's *activity* in Christ. Such a shift of interest is illustrative of the essential difference in the mythic structure of the two cultures, Semitic and Hellenistic; the latter is harmonic and tends toward the static with an emphasis upon *being*, while the former is dynamic and creative with a stress upon *acting* or *doing*.

The resurrection of Jesus belongs to the mythic structure of the Old Testament affirmation in quite the same sense as those aspects of his birth and origin which we discussed previously, but it belongs there for a slightly different reason. The earliest Christian proclamations about Jesus center around what is summed up as the resurrection; the resurrection is not, however, in these earliest proclamations what it has now come to mean for us. Because Jesus preached the nearness of God's eschatological act of bringing history to an abrupt close, he was put to death by the Roman authority at the behest of the Jewish Sanhedrin in Jerusalem. The first *Christological* evalua-

tion of his life and message was that he was the forerunner of
God's eschatological agent, the Son of Man. It was not long,
however, before the small band of his followers identified him
with this Son of Man (cf. Acts 3:12-26, especially vs. 19-21).
As the Son of Man *yet to come*, Jesus was considered to be in
the presence of God whither he had been taken by God. Step
by step the early community expanded this understanding of
God's having exalted Jesus until the complete cycle of events
was evolved in which the resurrection refers *only* to his having
been raised *from the dead*. The liturgical detailing of the
events surrounding the few days before and just after his death
are a product of the later church and do not reach into the
earliest strata of the church's history.

The expression " from the dead " does not mean " from
death " but " from among the dead ones." What it meant to
say was that unlike the ordinary Jew who dies and rests in a
sort of limbo among the shades, Jesus was immediately raised
to the right hand of God upon his death. This is the meaning
of the earliest proclamation of Jesus as the *raised Lord*. As the
story is expanded through liturgical rehearsal, details are added
and a transposition of interest sets in so that he is first *raised
from the grave*. This statement is then slightly altered so that
he *rises from the grave*. The ascension then becomes the means
whereby he is raised to the presence of God after having been
raised from the grave. Thus, the raising of Jesus becomes a
two-act drama; but this occurs only after a detailing of what
" from the dead " means in terms of subsequent experience of
the presence of the raised Lord. As in the case of the virgin
birth, the emphasis first shifts from an act of God involving
Jesus as the object of that act, to an act of Jesus involving himself, and finally to a datum of the natural order. The parallel to
the virginity of the mother of Jesus is the empty tomb; both
are on the level of a datum of the natural order and are far
from the mind of the early Christian community. The reason
for the shift of emphasis from history to nature is to be found
in the shift of the milieu in which the proclamation is made

from the Semitic to the Hellenistic world. As the virgin birth is no assertion about the physical status of a Hebrew maiden, so the resurrection gives no information about a hole in the ground on the outskirts of Jerusalem.

From thence he shall come to judge the quick and the dead. At the other end of the historical continuum envisaged in the mythic structure of the Biblical narrative is the *eschaton,* the end of history; it is the polar complement of the creation. As it was conceived in the theological outlook of the community leaders who were responsible for the Old Testament, the *eschaton* was the point toward which the world was developing and the one at which a judgment would be made by God. At first, of course, the judgment involved only Israel, but as the community experienced more history and was itself the object of God's judgment in the course of that history, a more mature and inclusive eschatology evolved. There was not, as we have already seen, a dogmatically structured eschatology that was universally accepted in all parts of Judaism. The one dogma was that God would bring history to a close with a judgment. For some groups, the judgment meant approbation for them and destruction for the rest; to others it meant a time of testing when God would reward those who had suffered unjustly in his cause. To still others it meant the vindication of God's inscrutable pattern of dealing with all men regardless of their membership in the Israelite community.

As the Israelite viewpoint was affected by Hellenistic thought, one of the more difficult problems posed by eschatology was, "What then?" Speculation as to what would happen after the end was part of popular piety, but it was never officially countenanced among those who held fast to the mythic structure involved in the doctrine of creation. One answer to the question of "What then?" is attempted, if not altogether successfully, by the author of the book of Revelation. He cannot avoid the reality of time, however, for he concentrates upon the thousand-year kingdom which will be enjoyed by the Christian martyrs *before* the final windup of history and the advent of judgment. What little he has to say about the "then" after the judgment may be an index of the difficulty of characterizing such a period when time ceases. The nature of the problem is quite simple despite the fact that the simplicity of the problem really complicates a solution to it; it depends upon the basic myth within which the Bible is conceived.

Time begins with the creation and ends with the *eschaton;* time is real, however, and it is as difficult to conceive, within this myth, of any time or history after the *eschaton* as it is to conceive of any time or history before the creation. The Greek myth of generality, in which time and space are ultimately unreal, could propose an answer to the question, but that answer would be discontinuous with the creation-*eschaton* myth in which time and space are not only real but in fact the only reality. It is quite revelatory that practically all of the Christian imagery used to depict heaven and hell, those states beyond the "then" of judgment, stems from classical Greco-Roman mythology and not primarily from the Biblical myth. This is an outstanding instance of the fusion that has taken place between Hellenistic thought and Biblical thought.

There may be a tragic flaw in the mythic structure of Biblical thinking at precisely this point of the time versus eternity struggle. The tardiness in developing as systematic an eschatology as their doctrine of creation may point to a real weakness in the entire Biblical outlook, but the fusion of the creation-*eschaton* myth with the myth of generality which undergirded Hellenistic thinking destroys the Biblical myth, for the one is oriented toward nature and evades time while the other is oriented toward history and takes time in all seriousness. Each of these two mythic structures is like a living organism; parts of one grafted upon the other are attacked and destroyed by the host. It is no solution of the basic problem to assume the timeless Greek myth as basic while allowing the Hebraic myth of time to govern only the segment of time which exists between creation and the *eschaton.* This is precisely what is done when a picture of heaven or of hell is drawn as the final chapter of the Biblical myth of the end.

(I believe in) *the Holy Ghost; the holy catholic church; the communion of saints; the forgiveness of sins; and the life of the age to come.* One of the ways in which we can arrive at some solution to the problem presented by the myth of creation-*eschaton* is by way of the Biblical myth itself. An essential factor in the Biblical myth is the existence of the community. For Israel, it was the chosen and elect people, but for the Christian community this image was extended to make room for the universalistic *populus Dei* called the *ekklēsia tou Theou* (the called out and elect people of God). This community for the Christian viewpoint was a new act of God. It was the locus of the continuing operation of the act of God in Christ, but it was also the field of concentration of the work of the Spirit. In effect, these two notions say the same thing: the church became the center whence emanated the continuing effect of God's recreative act in Christ. Consequently, when the creed lumps together a number of phrases loosely attached in the final paragraph of this affirmation, we must see in this catena of phrases a number of aspects of the same activity of God.

All of these phrases are attached, however loosely, to the Third Person of the Holy Trinity, the Holy Spirit. Each of them is a way of looking at the *ekklēsia*, although the viewpoint from which they look differs slightly in each case. The holy community is separated out for a mission; from its center the power of God once for all (*ephapax*) active in Christ for redemption continues to pour forth. As the locus of continuous operation of the act of God, the church is like an electromagnetic field; the Holy Spirit pervades the church but is effective *through* the church as a redemptive force toward the world. The church is also called the *fellowship of the holy ones,* i.e., communion of saints; "holy" does not mean "pious," however, but gets its meaning from *qadhosh* (Isa. 6:3). It preserves the notion of being separated *for*. Seen from another vantage point, the church is the community that has experienced the ultimate in God's mercy, his forgiveness of past self-centered-

ness. The opposite side of this experience is that of the possibility of a new beginning in life *for* God rather than *for* self.
As this community views its life, it stands between one eschatological act of God in Christ as expressed in the life, death,
and raising of Jesus and another as expressed in the images of
the Second Coming of Jesus as the Judge. The crux of the
problem is located here, for it can be seen as a question: Has
the *eschaton* already come, or is it yet to come?

Like a great number of either/or questions, this one can be
resolved in terms of the Biblical myth by an answer of both/
and. On the one side of the issue, it is clear that the early
church meant to answer the question by affirming the former
alternative; to designate Jesus as Messiah, translated as Christ,
is surely tantamount to saying either that the Messianic Age
has already begun to dawn or that it has indeed come. Such
an affirmation involves a tremendous alteration in one aspect
of the eschatological myth, however, for if the end has already
come with the advent of Jesus, what can be said of the life of
the community and the world that still continues?

The Fourth Evangelist demonstrates how this question was
eventually answered by calling the life of the church the " life
of the age (that was) to come "; in this respect he runs parallel
to Paul's handling of the question as well as to that of the
author to the Hebrews. Although the Fourth Evangelist seems
to come very close to suppressing the myth of the *eschaton*
in favor of a quasi-Gnostic myth, he has actually given us good
evidence of the transitional period during which the act of
God in Christ was being transferred from the notion of a purely
final act to a notion of a new beginning. At times also, even
Paul seems to succumb to a kind of mysticism. With his declaration concerning being " in Christ," he shows us a much
earlier stage of the same sort of thought as that indicated in
the Fourth Evangelist; he too tries to keep in tension the notion
of God's act in Christ as an eschatological act without suppressing the idea of complete finality which is yet to come.

The clue to this difficulty is contained in that stratum of

the New Testament in which the orientation is almost totally in the direction of a future coming of Jesus as Christ to judge the world and bring history to a close. The historical explanation that best answers the problem raised here is that we have already suggested. To repeat, the earliest evaluation of Jesus after his crucifixion was that he had died as the forerunner of the eschatological figure, the Son of Man. The first Christological evaluation of his life and its meaning was that he was, in fact, identical with the Son of Man and that he would soon come in that role. At this point the myth of the *eschaton* is still intact; it is still in complete agreement with the eschatology of Judaism. The second step in the Christological evaluation of Jesus took place when his death was viewed as Messianic. This stage of the evolution of Christology implied that the church was already living on the other side of the *eschaton,* which is patently impossible in terms of the Jewish eschatological myth. The structure of the myth was saved, however, by a process of reorienting the eschatological scheme. The life and death of Jesus were still viewed as eschatological, that is to say, they were in a very real sense a *final* act, *the* final act. Yet, the end of history was still to come, for the eschatological act was made a new act of creation. This was possible on Jewish grounds, for it grew out of the same mythic structure that permitted the Pentateuchal expansion backward from Abraham through Noah to Adam; each of the latter events was an end, but it produced a new beginning.

What ultimately saved the eschatological myth from complete destruction by designating the life and death of Jesus as eschatological was the introduction of a doctrine of "two ages," which arose through the reflection of certain apocalyptists upon the relation between the creation myth and the myth of the end. Among one school of thought, a correlation of the two myths was achieved by way of a new mythic concept of "*re*-creation." This new mythic structure affected the thinking of several early Christian writers, and its effect is to be felt to a considerable extent in Paul, the author of Hebrews,

and the author of Revelation among the New Testament
writers, while it achieves something approaching systematic
statement in Irenaeus (*Against the Heresies* IV. xxxviii).[51]

The origin of this derived myth is to be traced back into the
Old Testament, although its precise origins are not easy to
locate. Tributaries to it are to be found in the doctrine of the
remnant and the prophecy of the new covenant (Jer. 31:31).
The reoriented myth was itself born out of an earlier view of
the finality of God's judgment; the return of the exiled Israelites was reflected upon by the poet of the return whom we
know as the second Isaiah. As this myth was made a vehicle
for replacing the earlier myth of the Day of the Lord, so in the
Christian picture this new myth reoriented the earlier view,
but it could not replace it entirely.

The doctrine of the two ages gave the church a terminology
in which the period between the coming of Jesus in flesh and
the second Coming could be described. The Hebrew word for
"age" was 'olam, which was translated into Greek by aiōn;
the Greek adjective formed from this noun was aionios (per-
taining to the age or of the age). Consequently, the Greek
expression which is rendered "life of the age to come" or "life
everlasting" really means "life in the church." Once this expression gained currency in the Greek speaking world, however, it was easy to translate it into vita aeterna, the Latin
expression for "eternal life"; this translation is already an indication that in the Hellenistic world, the specifically Hebrew
idea contained in zōē aionios (life of the age to come) was
being interpreted in terms of another mythic structure, viz.,
the Greek myth of generality.

The Christian resolution of the problem contained in its
reoriented eschatology is not essentially a comfortable one, for
despite the fact that in Jesus Christ the "new creation" has
taken place, the church still clings to its earlier affirmation
that there is an end yet to come. All of the problems inherent
in the Jewish expectation of "the end" and the earlier Christian expectation of the Advent of Jesus in the role of Messiah

are still presented by the retention, within the mythic structure, of the basic Biblical myth of the end. To the extent that the church has kept this feature of the myth, it has exhibited its tenacity to maintain its essentially mythic orientation. It is clear, then, that the proclamation of Jesus as Messiah (the Christ) upset the framework of the myth, but very soon the myth righted itself and enfolded the new insight within its total outlook. Thus, we are still dealing, in the Christian proclamation, with a mythic structure that is essentially Hebrew — it does not permit the entrance of the timeless forever. No solution that incorporates the idealistic structure of the myth of the eternal can do justice to the Christian myth.

In this and the preceding section, it has been our intention to set forth the primary features of the Biblical Christian myth descriptively and historically without necessarily making an exhaustive analysis. We have attempted to probe the semantic structure of the myth in its contextual totality. Although we have used both the descriptive and historical techniques, we have tried to observe the principle that description precedes historical generalization. It is this principle, we believe, that has permitted us to see the more clearly the distinctive feature of the myth. In order to bring this analysis together and to give it direction, we should attempt to derive the semantic of this structure of expression. Therefore, we shall devote the following brief section to some generalizations about what we have here observed in the hope that these summary observations may be suggestive of a logic governing that historical type of mythic expression in which the Christian revelation is cast.

C. A Logic of Historical Myth?

Logic has been described as a normative science, one that prescribes the norms that guide the mind to correctness of thought. We might construe this description in such a way that it means that logic deals with the "laws" of thought. The burgeoning interest in psychological research has taught us, however, that this is not a very adequate understanding of the function of logic. A refinement of this description might insist that logic tells us how thinking *should* proceed rather than how it *does*. Yet, even this modification leaves the field of logic too large and vague. Our thought processes are not really stimulated by subjecting them to an ideal pattern or process. In fact, the creative activities of thought take place along a devious path rather than on a wide and well-marked highway. The most creative thinkers are frequently, if not always, the most erratic in their thinking activities. The means whereby the genius is separated from the maniac is not in the processes of his thinking but in what he produces.

Logic, as a normative science, is concerned to separate truth from error in the products of our thinking. Hence it is a formulation of the norms by which we judge the thoughts we have to be correct or in error. We should be inclined, however, to characterize logic as the touchstone of thinking.[52] Thus it would be viewed as a formalized collection of principles describing the connections that may properly exist among the propositions or elements of a language. This observation seems to parallel another to the effect that within a language (*langue*), several logics may be operative according to the vocabulary structure of its users.

For a considerable period of time since the days of Aristotle's *Organon*, logic was synonymous with deductive logic. Even today, in a good many colleges and universities, logic is taught on the basis of this assumption, although the number of places where this is the case is thankfully decreasing. Syllogistic reasoning still has its proper place, but it also has its severe limitations. Not the least of these limitations concerns the meaning of universal propositions. If the universal proposition is a tautology, that is to say, if it is true by definition, then a particular proposition derived from it adds no new knowledge. Perhaps the most widely used system employing deductive logic is Euclidean geometry, a highly abstract system originally devised for the measurement of inaccessible distances. Until the

Renaissance, however, deductive logic governed practically all areas of inquiry, including science as well as theology.

The Renaissance mind gave birth to the *Novum Organum,* the "new *Organon,*" which represented Bacon's attempt to turn science's attention from deductive reasoning to observation and experiment. The basic principles of this "new Aristotle" were expanded into a methodological manifesto in John Stuart Mill's *A System of Logic, Ratiocinative and Inductive: Being a Connected View of the Principles of Evidence and the Methods of Scientific Investigation,* first published in 1845, and now available in its eighth edition.

Thus, by the middle of the last century a new set of "criteria of validity" had been developed alongside the old. These criteria were rooted in empirical observation and pointed the way of generalization from particular instances to so-called *laws.* The reign of the laboratory method in scientific pursuits has only infrequently meant that students of science were articulately aware of Mill's canons of induction, but they knew how to use them even if they remained unaware of Mill's formal statement of these canons. Philosophers who were conversant with the criteria underlying the method of induction have not always been as sure of the validity of the method as its practitioners. One of these critics, Bertrand Russell, has made some astute observations about scientific method although he remains convinced of its usefulness, provided its limitations are appreciated. Because of certain formal fallacies inherent in it, Russell has doubts about the general validity of the inductive method. He is also deeply aware of the difficulty involved in the passage by way of inference from what has been experienced to what has not yet been experienced. His most significant objection goes to the core of what an inductive inference actually says. Granting that it is possible to make observations about what is not yet experienced, Russell indicates that these inferences are so abstract that they do not give all the information they appear to give.[53]

The breakdown of scientific trust in the "immutable laws

of nature," the occurrence of phenomena which broke open
the closed, causally structured universe, and the entirely
changed outlook of scientific thought since the advent of
quantum mechanics have contributed to a decrease of the
certainty that accompanied scientific research until a few short
decades ago. The critical modern scientist, whose predecessor did so much to develop the logic of induction, has
come to realize that less and less of what he deals with is
datum and more and more is inference; yet the canons upon
which his inferences rest are themselves seen as assumptions,
however practical they may seem.

One type of proposition with which neither the logic of
deduction nor the logic of induction has been able adequately
to deal is what is known as the " singular " proposition. History
is discussed, however, in terms of singular propositions — of
the sort " Julius Caesar crossed the Rubicon." Historical inference is based upon this sort of proposition. Deductive logic
tried to distribute singular or historical propositions between
universal and particular propositions according to the degree
of generality represented in them. The logic of induction, when
it treated such propositions at all, handled them as particulars;
the result of this method was that kind of historical writing
which under the influence of inductive logic became a quest
for generality in history.

The mythic type of assertion with which we have been concerned in this chapter belongs to the class of singular propositions. The historical events in which Israelites and Christians
alike had been encountered by Yahweh were always expressed
in singular propositions. The mythic statements by which Israel
as well as the Christians oriented themselves to the world in
terms of those singular historical events were also cast in the
form of singular propositions. The logic of deduction cannot
comfortably handle such propositions, nor can the logic of induction; therefore, unless they are pure nonsense, these singular propositions must exhibit a logic of their own. A clue to
the sort of logic involved in these statements as they are re-

lated to one another is to be found in Wittgenstein's *Tractatus Logico-Philosophicus*, to which we referred previously in the second chapter. The *Tractatus* is a quite unorthodox work that looks, at first sight, like a collection of sentential wisdom. Were it not for the quite prosaic quality of its successive propositions, the reader might be tempted to think that it is intended to be poetry. Unless he pays some quite strict attention to the convention employed by the author, the reader is sure to decide that the book resembles *Poor Richard's Almanack* more than a unified treatise on logic. In order to relate the propositions to one another, Wittgenstein devised an intricate system of sequential and subordinate numeration. The system assigns to each proposition a clearly defined position in the total context. One might say that this system accomplishes its purpose in a way far superior to ordinary discourse. By means of Arabic numerals decimally distinguished, the total view is never lost when a proposition is quoted from the *Tractatus;* thus, for example, proposition 6.51 precedes proposition 6.52, and both are parallel in value, but propositions 6.521 and 6.522, equal in value to each other, follow 6.52 and are subordinate to it. Wittgenstein depends entirely upon this expressive and revealing numeration system to expose the fabric of interrelation in this work. He eschews the convention of related paragraphs containing related sentences such as one normally finds in connected discourse. This method of relating separate propositions resembles rather closely an unexpanded skeletal outline, but it is more expressive than ordinary discourse.

Generally the *Tractatus* has been recognized as the foundation work of that philosophy in which the principle of verification plays so large a part, that is, logical empiricism. A closer reading of this enigmatic work appears to justify the contention that its author attempted to establish a fundamental distinction between what can be *said* discursively and what can only be *shown* in such language.[54] The key proposition for such an interpretation of Wittgenstein's purpose says precisely that (proposition 4.1212). Since Wittgenstein devotes a number of propositions to this distinction, it seems hard to avoid the conclusion that he was as much interested in what must be *shown* as in what can be *said*. He calls the inexpressible the "mystical" (proposition 6.522), but he also indicates that this is precisely the matter with which the important problems of life are involved (propositions 6.52, 6.521). In this regard, he approaches the poetic and resembles the existentialist.

It is quite possible to maintain that Wittgenstein considered the things that could not be said as nonlogical or even illogical (and therefore nonsense?), provided that we mean by "logic" the Frege-Russell symbolic logic in which logicians deal with such problems as the foundations of mathematics. Nevertheless, he does apparently limit the problems that can be solved by this logic to those which are scientific (proposition 6.52), while the problems of life fall outside that category. Since the problems of science are problems in nature, the problems of life seem to fall into the category of history. From this, a further inference could be made to the effect that the problems of life cannot be expressed in the mathematical logic peculiar to scientific reasoning. We have before us in the religious and theological assertions of the Hebrew-Christian community a set of propositions interested in the "problems of life." If we were to invert Wittgenstein's statement, it would result that what can only be shown, in Frege-Russell terms, could be said if we were to stick to the category of history. In other words, it would appear that we have mutually exclusive systems of expression: in one, questions of nature can be *said*, but other questions can only be *shown*; in the other, questions of history can be said, but others only shown.

For each of these systems of expression, a distinct logic seems to be required; what must be avoided is the confusion of these logics with one another. Thus, it will be necessary for us to recognize that the logic peculiar to the language of science is a valid logic and has significance in questions where nature is the fundamental or prime category. In this regard, we do well to hearken to the linguistic analysts who have analyzed propositions so meticulously and have so well clarified the relationship among the statements on the logic of nature, deductive and inductive. On the other hand, as the burgeoning discipline of historical study amply demonstrates, there is a logic of historical inference which deals primarily in singular propositions, the material of which the prime category is unique and unrepeatable history. Here we can only point to pioneers rather than to a body of assured results. The logic of historical inference is yet to be organized into canons, but this will have to be done by scholars who are prepared to deal creatively with the singular proposition.

The lines along which the development of a historical logic must take place are, in so many ways, only poorly blazed trails. As we read and interpret the blazes and markers, we find them cast in terms of singulars and uniques. In terms of the only logic we really know by virtue of our Greco-Roman intellectual heritage, the canons will be largely negative. Thus we shall have to make our way through the phase of negativity to a positive and affirmative ground. We cannot begin by establishing criteria any more than Aristotle or Mill could have done had they lived centuries before their time. Therefore, our aims for the present must be less ambitious. Some characteristics of the categories basic to such a logic are at least evident; the most important of them is that the categories cannot be drawn in terms of the structure of the Greek language. If these categories must be drawn in terms of the structure of a language family, perhaps the best source is that language in which the historico-mythic expression came to fruition, the Semitic. Particularly in Hebrew, a structural analysis will show a predominance of the verbal expression over the nominal. Metalinguistically, Hebrew shows a character of event-consciousness, which is primary for a logic of history. Perhaps, however, the philosophical turn taken by the philosophy of science will be a source of useful direction; in the philosophy of process, *event* is a prime category. In either case, the emphasis is upon the dynamic and the emergent, a characteristic that is most useful for a logic of mythico-historical expression.

Another negatively stated observation about the formal development of this logic is that abstraction must be eschewed. Part of our difficulty in attempting to understand the logical behavior of the mythic language in which the Hebrew-Christian revelation is couched has been an unfortunate polarity that has grown up involving the terms "abstract" and "concrete." The concrete does not permit abstraction; abstraction from concrete terms is simply illegitimate. When a term is concrete, it is a historical term; when it is treated by means of abstraction, it is no longer seen as a concrete term but becomes particular — and "particular" belongs in the logic whose categories are in terms of nature. This does not imply that we may no longer treat concrete terms as particulars, but it does mean that we must recognize that we are doing so and be guided accordingly. The logical classification of singulars as propositions about classes of one member is an honest attempt to deal with concreteness by way of a logic that is not ideally suited for concrete expressions. On the whole, this approach seems to be a frank admission that singulars simply do not fit into this logical system. At the same time, in the logic of mythico-historical expression, universals would appear to be equally difficult to deal with. Universals rest upon abstraction and abstraction is not at home in the structural semantic of mythic expression.

In another vein, somewhat closely related, the whole structure of causality appears to be a surd in the logical system toward which we are striving. Cause is a characteristic attributed to natural phenomena, but even in this reality of things its total sway has been threatened considerably by the results of recent research in astrophysics and psychology.[55] There is nothing particularly novel about the contention that causality is inadequate as a framework for interpreting historical phenomena, but perhaps we shall yet come to a deeper apprehension of the scope and meaning of this observation.

Does the picture that we have only delineated in outline here mean that science and theology, or perhaps science and religion, cannot speak *to* each other? Not in the least! Each will have to understand the logic with which the other operates, however, before some fruitful interchange is possible. There are two alternatives open to those who would bridge the gulf; one is the devising of a metalanguage, and the other is translating. A metalanguage that would embrace both logics would be as difficult to handle as any other artificial language; it would also present the problem of learning such a language. Theoretically, such an artificial language might be of great assistance, but we hardly know enough about *general* scientific theory to develop those areas where nature and history are tangent to each other, that is, in the human sciences such as psychology and anthropology. Gestalt psychology promises a lead here, but we are hardly sure enough of method for achieving trustworthy insight into specifically human life and endeavor.

The aims of translation are more modest. This approach takes serious account of the present isolation of one field of inquiry from another which is a product of specialization and different focuses of attention. As there are those linguists who work toward a universal tongue, so there must be scientific generalists who strive toward general theory. In the meantime, the most effective work will be accomplished by those who attempt to interpret the idiom of one structure to those oriented toward another. This is the less glorious path, but it is a more relevant one at the moment.

Translation is fraught with perils, however, and not all translators are sufficiently aware of the pitfalls that are so deceptively camouflaged in the path that they have chosen. Therefore, it is indicated that we should attempt to set forth the task of the translator in clear terms, and after having done so, to examine briefly but critically the results achieved by some of the better-known translators.

Chapter V

One Language to Another:
The Perils of Translation

One of the more distinctive accomplishments of the Protestant Reformation was the widespread translation of the Bible into the vernacular tongues of Europe. From sporadic beginnings before the Reformation, this movement toward translation reached a high point in the production of standard versions of the Bible in the greater traditions within Reformation Christianity. Lutherans, Calvinists, and Anglicans, all produced distinctive translations of the Bible for the use not only of the clergy but of the laity as well. It was not very long, however, before these standard versions acquired a place of veneration in the various churches with the result that they became classics. The vocabulary employed in the translations tended to wed them to a past era making necessary some fresh rendering into the rapidly altering language of the majority of church members. While the Bible in the vernacular tongue of a past age continued to occupy a position of primacy, this translation function was performed by preachers whose education included some firsthand knowledge of the original text of the Bible. In time, however, revisions of the standard translations were called for. When these revisions were undertaken, both the language into which translation was to be made and the documents to be translated had undergone some change.

Of the changes in vernacular tongues we need say but little. To the student of English literature, the rate of change in the English language since the sixteenth century is a well-known fact. For one less well versed in the characteristics of linguistic change, a comparison of the Sunday morning lesson read from the Authorized Version with the language employed by the preacher in his sermon will demonstrate the magnitude of the change that has taken place in some three and a half centuries. On the other side of the picture, it must be emphasized that nineteenth-century discoveries of manuscripts wrought a profound effect upon our understanding of the nature of the Biblical record. Where it used to be assumed that the Bible was a more or less static quantity that had been faithfully guarded through transmission in all its details, the development of the discipline of textual criticism has shown that the text of the Bible is more like a broad river into which have flowed several tributaries. The Latin Bible used throughout the Middle Ages was only one of the many streams that made up this broad river; the Greek and Hebrew texts employed by the translators of the Authorized Version were likewise only partially representative of a much broader tradition.

The breadth of the textual tradition of the Bible was emphasized even more by studies in the various ancient versions of the text. A modern critical text of the Old and New Testaments together with an *apparatus criticus* outlines the many-sided history of textual transmission which was practically unknown two centuries ago. It also illuminates the distinct change in the text that is to be translated. While this change does not affect the over-all message of the Bible, it does decidedly alter our understanding of it in many details.

Meanwhile, historical and critical studies in various areas added measurably to our understanding of the ancient world. The ancient Near East, the classical and Hellenistic West, the history and philosophy of religions, and the structure of the Hebrew-Christian religious tradition have all been subjected to deep analysis not only by distinctly Christian scholars but by others as well. As a result we have a much more illuminated view both of the gospel and the world to which it was addressed; hence, the peculiar character of the Christian challenge to the Greco-Roman world is now understood in a much profounder way than the Reformers understood either the ancient world or the challenge of the gospel to this world. A clear manifestation of the altered stance of modern Protestantism is its revivified concern for the place of liturgy in the totality of the Christian witness. The problem of translating the Christian gospel has assumed much larger proportions because the task of translation is appreciated in greater depth. The translator is no longer free to render word for word a literature that is distinctly religious and in part theological into a language that will alter the semantic structure of that literature beyond recognition.

A. The Task of Translation

Etymologically, the words " translate " and " transfer " are derived from the same Latin verb unit. Those who suffered through the wearying drills designed to ensure that Latin students would learn the principal parts of verbs will recall, even if without relish, that the " irregular " verb *ferre* had what appeared to be the oddest forms in the perfect tense. *Tuli* and (*t*)*latus* could hardly be more remote from *ferre;* but comfort was derived from the realization that " went " is no more closely related to " go " or " gone." Even a mere beginner in Latin knows that the aim of translating is to " carry " what is said in one language " across " to another language. What is frequently missed by beginners in translation — and not infrequently missed continually by practicing translators — is that no translator is ever able to perform this task to perfection. Something is always dropped on the way over, or else something is picked up on the way over.

The most difficult problem for a polyglot, i.e., one who is familiar with more than one tongue,[56] is the translation of a selection of speech or written language from one tongue to another. With the aid of a lexicon, he can convey the sense of words, and by utilizing the further assistance of reference grammars, he is also able to convey the sense of phrases and

clauses into another tongue. Nevertheless, the translator stands
as a mediator between two speech communities. The degree
of success with which he can mediate will be determined by
the facility he has in understanding the medium of expression
used by the community from which he translates as well as that
of the community to which he translates. As a very simple but
illuminative instance of this fact we may cite the *Dialogues* of
Plato. The *Dialogues* are not really understood, even in Greek,
apart from the historical and intellectual climate in which
they were written and without some basic understanding of
the questions being asked in fifth-century Athens to which this
form of discourse and its content were a relevant attempt at
an answer.[57] The translator of the *Dialogues* must appreciate
this dimension of the original in its own context. On the other
hand, he must be sufficiently aware of the tongue to which
he translates so that he may avoid as many misconceptions as
possible.

Frequently, the specialist in classical literature is more at
home in the total viewpoint of Greek than in the vocabulary
structure of his contemporaries in his native language. Thus,
what we have called a "literal" translation may often fail to
convey the precise significance of the original specifically because of the semantic structure of the two tongues. Translation
becomes as much an art as original composition when this dimension of the task is appreciated.

The problem becomes even more acute in rendering the epic,
didactic, and dramatic poetry which embodied the mythic
structure of classical thought. Homer, Hesiod, and the Tragedians present a peculiar difficulty for the translator because
this literature was not merely the poetry of Greece; it was
akin to what we have come to know as sacred literature and
provided the vehicle whereby the orientation of the Greek
culture was expressed. Between the philosophic development
represented in Plato and the Academy, carried on through
Aristotle and the Lyceum, and the dramatic expression
achieved in the Tragedians there was a profound conflict. As

Greek thought developed, this conflict was submerged rather than resolved. In the end the neater formulations of the philosophers triumphed as the characteristic contribution of the Greeks to their heirs and successors. Only more recently with the advent of a philosophy of existence has the subordinated Dionysiac religious consciousness that lies beneath the tragic poetry of the Greek dramatists found any real point of contact in translation for Western man. The reasons for this may lie as much in the failure of the translators to appreciate the tragic dimension of this aspect of Greek expression as in the changed mental outlook of our own culture. Perhaps the source of the lack of communication in this regard is to be located among philosophers and literary savants who would not regard themselves as translators primarily. We cannot avoid the fact that our understanding of classical culture comes at least as much from philosophers, historians, and other humanistic scholars as it does from the Hellenists and Latinists who have been forced to concentrate their attention upon language.

When we step across the line dividing Greek literature from the Semitic, we enter an entirely different world. The problems encountered by the translator of Hebrew are many times those of the translator of Greek. In one sense, the well-oriented Hebraist is a much more vital link in the mediation between the Christian and Greek views of the world because these two speech forms have so very little in common. It is a shock to the beginner in Hebrew to realize that this language has no real interest in or means of expressing the notion of tense in verbs. To us who speak Indo-European dialects, this notion is absolutely necessary. Equally baffling to him is the distinction so finely drawn in the various forms of the Hebrew verb stem; here in differentiating among the light or simple stem, the intensive stem, and the causative stem, the Hebrew language presents a complete and distinctive semantic structure. This peculiarity must be reflected in translation despite the difficulties. Again, the exceptionally close relationship between noun stems and verb stems, the absence of a developed inflec-

tional system in the noun, and the peculiar way of stating relationship between two nouns are part of this total semantic
structure. We should consider it odd to alter the first noun in
the expression " son of Abraham "; in our language family, " of
Abraham " is a unit as the more highly inflected members of
the language family demonstrate by putting it into the geni-
tive. On the other hand, in Hebrew " son of " is the unit, and it
alters when followed by another noun which is not altered.
This peculiarity, as so many of the others we have here in-
stanced, can be considered merely morphological features, but
they contain within them a semantic dimension that cannot
be ignored.

At the syntactic level in Hebrew, another new world opens.
Even the casual reader of the Old Testament in translation is
familiar with the striking parallelism which suffuses so much of
Hebrew poetry. Immediately one recalls the words of the
psalmist:

> What is man that Thou dost constantly think of us?
> And the son of man that Thou dost worry over us?
> (Ps. 8:4.) [58]

Repetition with substitution of nearly synonymous words se-
cures at once an inner rhythm and an emphasis that are quite
foreign even to the vocabulary in which we write poetry. The
construction of a Hebrew sentence is another indication of
what we can call syntactical semantics. It might be possible to
charge this peculiarity in sentence construction, with the verb
appearing first or nearly so, to the fact that all languages exhibit idiosyncrasies in poetry, were it not true that we meet
the same feature in the soberest prose of Ezra in almost the
same profusion as in the lyrical raptures of The Psalms and
the Second Isaiah.

From the viewpoint of lexical semantics, we can examine the
Hebrew vocabulary to discover some of the problems facing
the translator. The great majority of Hebrew verbs and nouns
consist of triconsonantal units; depending upon how these com-

binations of consonants are vocalized, they produce nouns as
well as verbs. A further system of preformatives creates a large
portion of the remaining nouns in the vocabulary, while the
balance is made up of proper nouns derived from a number of
varied sources. Briefly, we can say that the Hebrew tongue is
essentially a verbal tongue as contrasted to the Indo-European
tongues, which are primarily nominal. Although this generalization might be misunderstood out of context, it is only fair
to say that it is made from the viewpoint of structural linguistics.

One of the most puzzling features of Hebrew for an Indo-
European speaker is the absence of the intransitive verb and
the so-called verb substantive. Intransitive verbs, such as
"rise," "sit," "lie," and "stand," take up a considerable portion
of our vocabulary, but in Hebrew, these notions are expressed
by means of a verb expressing completed *action*. For instance,
one *stands* in a place because he has *been stood* there, according to the Hebrew conception. This enigma is brought to its
epitome in the absence of the verb "to be" in the uses with
which we are most familiar – "the sun *is* red" – and consequently, a number of the problems of language inherent in our
tongue are simply nonexistent in Hebrew. That sort of sentence
in Greek which formed so much of the logical development
epitomized in Aristotle's *Organon* is simply inexpressible *as a
sentence* in Hebrew. When the verb that we translate "to be"
is used in Hebrew, it signifies *action* and *not status*. The nearest
we can come to a translation of the verb *hayah*, erroneously
translated by a form of "to be," is by using the verb "happen"
or, in some cases, "become."

From the philosophical viewpoint, these semantic peculiarities of the Hebrew tongue present a number of profound
difficulties. Most of them are already smoothed over in the
vernacular translations of the Old Testament because we hear
these books read in a tongue that enshrines all of our logical
presuppositions. That is to say, the semantic structure of English protrudes so definitely that we cannot very often perceive

the Hebrew semantic structure. Many generations of translators and revisers have not helped to keep the sharply Hebraic
quality of the Old Testament alive. In striving for intelligibility
many translators have, unwittingly in most cases, created an
entirely new semantic structure within the vernacular version
of the Bible.

The most effective translators in our day are not those who
render the text afresh but those who have responsibly striven to
expound and set forth in some systematic way what is called,
for better or for worse, Biblical theology. The titles of two relatively recent books show the shift in emphasis more convinc-
ingly than a hundred pages of exposition could ever do. One
of these books, by E. L. Mascall, is entitled *He Who Is: A Study
in Traditional Theism.*[59] This is an admirable exposition of a
theistic philosophy whose Greek orientation is recognized by
the author and succinctly stated in the formula " he who is,"
a phrase that is inexpressible in Biblical Hebrew, or in any
other Semitic tongue, for that matter. At the other pole is
G. Ernest Wright's *God Who Acts: Biblical Theology as Re-
cital.*[60] Dr. Wright catches and transmits the peculiar semantic
and the logic that underlies Hebraic expression in a clear and
brilliant exposition that emphasizes the mythico-historical
structure of Biblical, religious thought. Both of these books
are examples of translation at a level beyond the mere rendering of Biblical texts. One cannot help appreciating the timeli-
ness of Dr. Wright's book while noting a certain degree of
irrelevance in the scholastic terms used by Dr. Mascall. A more
extensive attempt at this sort of translation is provided by the
joint undertaking of Dr. Wright and Prof. Reginald H. Fuller.
This is a rendering of the entire panorama of Biblical history
entitled *The Book of the Acts of God.*[61]

The difficulties involved in translating from one language to
another are beginning to become more apparent, but they are
being treated as challenge rather than as obstacle. The classical philologists of an earlier era were preoccupied with getting
beyond the language in which the Bible was written in order

that they might expound the cultural ideas inherent in the literature. They suffered from an acute myopia, however, because of their presupposition that all cultures were concerned with the same or very similar questions. Structural linguists have helped to overcome a large part of the philologist's myopia, but the task which the philologist set for himself must continue to be prosecuted *through* the language rather than around it. Instead of bringing presuppositions to our translations as to what logic operates or should operate, we shall approach the documents as listeners to discover that logic. Thus, the task of translation means exegesis *before* translation rather than merely after. A translation will then be much closer to a paraphrase than to what we have commonly known as translations. The study of the Biblical languages will also be a somewhat different undertaking from what it has been in the past if we are to equip preachers as well as scholars to pursue the all-important project of translating for communication.

There is still another level at which translation must be pursued. It is not enough merely to set forth in its stark nakedness the peculiar idiom of the mythico-historical language of the Bible. Important as this task is, it is only a preliminary; it must be granted that it is an indispensable preliminary, but it remains preliminary. In one very real sense, the monumental undertaking of Karl Barth in his *Church Dogmatics* belongs at this preliminary level.[62] In another sense, of course, this undertaking has a finality to it, for the only task that remains is to "translate" the hearer into the context of this idiom so that he might participate in it. The aim and purpose of a work like Tillich's, as the title of his peculiar contribution demonstrates, is on a more advanced level than Barth's.

There is a world of difference between the task of the *dogmatic* theologian and that of the *systematic* theologian.[63] Dogmatic theology can orient us toward the center whence we understand ourselves and the church, but a church that is concerned only with self-understanding, of its individual members or of the corporate entity, has lost touch with the vital polarity of the Biblical doctrine of election. Yes, God has chosen and redeemed his church in Christ, but the church is redeemed *for* his service *to* his world. Here the mediatorial position of the church as translator comes to its full fruition as we partake of the culture that is the gospel and (cor) relate it in holistic terms through our participation in the whole of the created order as profitable servants of the creator. It is not enough to be satisfied with *my salvation;* unless the affirmation is related to the total structure of reality as it is conceived by the most capable and responsible observers inside or outside the church, it is left to suspend in mid-air having no contact with that reality.[64]

Translating the Christian message is, then, a multiphasic undertaking. The primary step consists in a descriptive study of the language in which the proclamation is couched in its normative literature and its liturgy. A translation starting elsewhere belies the meaning of normative as it is applied to the canon of Scripture. In many ways, this is the most difficult step since it involves an abandoning of certain jealously guarded presuppositions, many of which are not articulately understood as presuppositions. The descriptive phase of analyzing the Biblical idiom must be accompanied by that sort of scientific impartiality which characterizes the approach of a linguistic scientist to a language whose structural and semantic system is unknown to him. From the descriptive to the historical phase, the pathway is precarious, but it is not unmarked. Historical analysis proceeds from the descriptive by drawing the line of change marked out between the stages and levels previously described. The generalizations that are drawn from the descriptive and historical analysis will assist in exposing the semantic structure which is peculiar to that mythic variety of thought in which the Hebrew and Christian scriptures abound. Only after these preliminary steps is it possible to undertake any actual linguistic translation of the documents that comprise the canon of Scripture.

Simultaneously, of course, the dogmatic-kerygmatic paraphrase of the documents as well as the symbols of the faith may be carried on, but both proceed from the same foundations in historical and descriptive study of the primary documents. The task is far from complete, however, until the *logical* and *semantic* conflict between the viewpoint oriented to history and that oriented to nature is frankly recognized, confronted, and dealt with. A careful and responsible attempt must be made to reconcile, correlate, and otherwise bring to a real confrontation with each other the categorical systems of nature and history in a systematic and creative thrust.

Each step in the translation process depends upon the cumulative results of all the preceding steps. As we trace these steps in reverse, we finally arrive at the normative level, which is the Biblical witness. It is incumbent upon each age to make a new translation of this normative stratum so that the message of the gospel may impinge upon the culture as kerygma and enter into dialogue with the culture as systematic theology. Hence, the history of the translation effort must be " re-enacted " in each generation in order to appreciate what was being done in each historical epoch. But this kind of study, which we have called " re-enactment," is more than mere review, for it must be critical study as well. New disciplines, new insights, and more effective methods of understanding what the normative level says will provide the basis for criticizing *what* was translated in each epoch, while an appreciation of the inner structure of the culture during each of these epochs will supply the standards for criticizing *how* the translation was carried through. Perhaps the most significant reason for continual review and revision of the foundational steps in the translation process is that one or more aspects of a previously viable structure tends to become fossilized in the present structure.

The translation effort is like a seamless robe that cannot be divided and retain its character. Therefore, the claim of dogmatic theologians, for example, to an autonomy that exempts their work from criticism by the most responsible results in the analysis of the normative literature of the Bible can only result in idolatrous worship of a formula rather than the God and Father of our Lord Jesus Christ. Once the critical attitude is permitted entrance into the theological perspective, its effect must be allowed to develop "without hindrance or let." The controls are exercised from the two poles that characterize the translation process. The one pole consists of the normative witness of the church's faith, and the other is to be found in the structure of the culture that is being addressed by the church. All else in between is simply a means to an end and subject to drastic revision as the situation demands.

A clearer understanding of the translator's task will eliminate the absurdity of dogmatic theologians' exerting pressure upon Biblical exegetes to arrive at results that must fit into present misunderstandings of yesterday's dogmatic formulations. The entire process of translation is constantly in flux, but it may not choose to anchor itself anywhere short of its proper foundation in the descriptive study of the normative documents of faith, the Scriptures. Even this descriptive study is not final, for it is constantly in process, and it is deictic in that it points beyond itself and the documents it studies to the religious affirmation of a specific historical community and thence to the God in whom alone we may put ultimate trust.

As we have suggested, translation is fraught with perils. These perils are indicated in some of the most successful attempts at translation, but they are underlined in the ways in which these attempts have been employed by the successors to the translators. One pole or the other is so frequently ignored that translation stagnates and the translator abandons his role as mediator to become polemist.

B. Translations and Translators

The course of the history of Christian thought can be traced by means of a line drawn through the crisis situations wherein the church has been challenged fundamentally on the grounds of its construct of itself and the world in which it exists, and has met those challenges constructively and creatively. Thus we can find the main direction of this history along the line that runs through Paul, the Hellenistic Jew transformed into Christian missionary; Athanasius, who was the object of bitter persecution but in the midst of it achieved a theological perspective that entitles him to recognition as one of the earliest systematic theologians, if not the earliest; and Augustine, the Neoplatonist rhetorician converted to the role of the first Christian philosopher. By the time of Augustine, Platonism was firmly entrenched in the Christian camp, and the theologians who followed Augustine had only to work out the details of the translation of which he had been the architect.

Christian Aristotelianism. The next great crisis came when the church was faced with the advent of Aristotelianism. When the newly discovered philosophical structure made its appearance, the systematic exposition of the church's affirmation in terms of Platonism had crystallized into a dogmatic theology. The alternatives were clearly defined: reject Aristotelianism in the name of a dogmatic Platonism, or seize the newly emerging viewpoint as a means for expounding the Christian gospel. Several attempts were made to translate the gospel into Aristotle's terms, but the majority of the church was content to shout answers from behind the protective walls of Platonism — answers that were irrelevant to the questions being asked by a world learning to use Aristotle's method. The completeness with which Thomas Aquinas rescued the church's proclamation from utter irrelevance by adapting the mediated Aristotelianism slowly emerging to the service of Christian apologetics needs no demonstration by us. Today, the name Thomism is practically synonymous with Christian Aristotelianism in a large segment of the church and designates the systematic translation of the Christian affirmation into the structure of Aristotelianism.

Despite the fact that the effort of Thomas is no longer considered more than a phase, albeit an important phase, in the history of translating the Christian affirmation, there are certain areas in the church where it is still treated as normative. Within Roman Catholic circles, it is the accepted framework in which theological thinking is pursued, and although there may be differences among the interpreters of Thomas, this is the structure that has the explicit support of the *magisterium* of the Roman Catholic Church.[65] Some philosophers and some theologians of Roman Catholic obedience have explored the philosophy of existence; most notable among these is Gabriel Marcel, whose theological views could hardly be said to have had the approval, much less the hearty endorsement, of the Holy See.[66] Outside the Roman obedience, the method that resulted from "baptizing" Aristotle still holds a mysterious power over Christian minds. Many who use this system would not recognize their orientation as Aristotelian and would probably be shocked to discover that they were thinking in a "Thomistic" way. What we mean by this is that some form of the cosmological argument for the existence of God is assumed in principle if not articulately. Certain advantages have been claimed for the cosmological argument, but whether it is the strictly cosmological argument or the more commonly used cosmological-teleological argument, the outlook embodied in it is singularly inappropriate for purposes of mid-twentieth-century translation.

Apart from the fact that this argument for the existence of God provided an answer, in Aristotelian terms, to a question that was asked not by Aristotle but by the Scholastic theologians who adapted his outlook, modern crypto-Aristotelians do not really make it clear that they understand the question to which the cosmological-teleological argument was an answer. The medieval philosophical theologian was not interested in *proving* the existence of God, but he was concerned to answer the question, How is it possible to believe in the God of Christian proclamation in the light of increasing knowledge about the structure of reality as described by Aristotelian science? The way in which this question was answered was by seizing upon the pattern of causality as exhibited in the regular patterns of the Aristotelian description of reality. Thus the medieval theologian was attempting to show, in the terms in which the question was asked, that it was not incompatible with the assumed structure of reality to believe in the God who is encountered in Christian experience. The use of the Aristotelian structure was dictated, however, by its general acceptance among those who would question the validity of the Christian affirmation. This simple fact is not infrequently misunderstood both by Christians who continue to employ the Aristotelian structure and by those scientists and philosophers who confuse this structure with the Christian outlook.

In the environment where Christians assume the Aristotelian structure, consciously or otherwise, and scientists object to the importation of an unnecessary assumption, the scientist is closer to the truth than the uncritical Christian apologist who continues to point to regularities of nature as "evidence" for the existence of God. The scientist rightly demands that the Christian spokesman clarify what he means by "evidence" and why he will not accept negative evidence as militating against his thesis that God exists.[67] The misuse of the Aristotelian structure as a vehicle for translating the Christian message results in rejection of the Christian proclamation by scientists, philosophers, and humanists simply because they do not accept an Aristotelian structure of reality. They conclude that the Christian message must be bound to a metaphysic of substance and attribute.

When the argument from miracle is introduced into this context, it confuses the issue even further because the scientist is led to believe that the Christian apologist is making an assertion about natural phenomena about which, as scientist, he is admittedly more capable of making assertions and judging them also. The logician who appreciates the mythico-historical structure in which the religious language of the church is conceived knows that this rejection by the scientist is right. The Christian who makes an assertion about miracle as though he were discussing natural (or supernatural) phenomena is introducing a mythico-historical category untranslated into the logic of nature. Thus, an attempt to "translate" on these grounds is tantamount to a refusal to translate because it does not reckon with the environment out of which the translation is to be made. Such an attitude does not come to terms with the fact that Christian faith can never be bound to any single philosophical system.[68]

An important shortcoming of any approach to a doctrine of God through nature is that if it works at all, it works as well for deism as for theism. The cosmological approach is causal in outlook. The Greek word *kosmos* means " order," primarily, and it derives its second meaning " world " from a specific view of reality. Aquinas appreciated that a properly Christian view of God could not be achieved by this route, a fact that accounts for his use of the term " revelation." For Thomas, knowledge of God attained through nature is *natural revelation;* unaided by *divine revelation,* man could not attain knowledge of God as he is known in Christian faith. The extra gift (*donum super-additum*) had to be bestowed by God; this divine revelation comes to fruition in the church through its own specific history. We overlook the great achievement of Thomas Aquinas *as a translator* if we disregard the fact that the categorical structure which he forged made it possible to speak the language of a world rapidly becoming accustomed to speaking in an Aristotelian mode. By developing the distinctions between natural theology and revealed theology, Thomas was a strong witness for the uniqueness of the Christian proclamation. It was as if he were to say that history, a specific history, is the category which distinguishes faith in the God and Father of our Lord Jesus Christ from philosophical theism.

In the theological development that ensued upon the post-Tridentine fracturing of the church, one of Thomas' categories, natural revelation or natural theology, ceased to be known as revelation or theology; the other, divine revelation or revealed theology, was the only one that kept the name of revelation. The resulting misconception of the faith versus reason problem is only too well known. With the detailing of a scientific cosmology in terms of natural law, the part of the Thomistic synthesis known as natural theology seemed to be vindicated. With this secularized view of natural theology, the argument for the existence of God could then be said, by those translating the Christian message, to have been established beyond reasonable doubt. Desiring to grant as much as possible, translators who worked from this standpoint tended to jettison the category of divine revelation, at least in terms of its being propositions imparted from outside the closed universe of nature. This method failed in the long run because it did not preserve the uniqueness of the Christian message which is guaranteed by the mythic structure of the Christian gospel. The Liberal movement of the nineteenth century had much to commend it for its eagerness to engage in the apologetic task, but it, too, failed because it dissociated itself from the mythic structure of the gospel.[69]

The breakdown of the natural law model of the universe in scientific research as well as from the standpoint of historical study has completed the bankruptcy of Christian Aristotelianism. Business still goes on at the old establishment, to be sure, but it is only a clearance sale before the premises are vacated. New emporia at different locations under other management are competing for the trade of those who would rather deal in a more trustworthy market. The philosophy of process and the philosophy of existence are on the frontiers today reaching for a more adequate understanding of the total situation revealed by scientific and historical research. These directions of philosophical thought nurtured by linguistic analysis on the one hand and the philosophy of symbolic form on the other constitute the environment in which serious philosophic thought is struggling for a responsible outlook. Consequently, any translation of the Christian message must be directed toward these inquiries, since they promise the most adequate view of the world that is likely to emerge from our current understanding of the character of nature and history. That is to say, we shall find one context, that to which we translate, in the philosophic generalizations now being made on the basis of the most responsible scientific and humanistic studies.

As we have already suggested, the other context, that *from* which we translate, must be understood in all its multiplicity of dimensions. We can no more translate a seventeenth-century " scientific " view of Christian origins into the twentieth-century nontheological context than we can presuppose seventeenth-century science and philosophy as forming the thought world into which the gospel must be translated. The sciences upon which we draw for a penetration into the early Christian thought world are likewise a gain belonging to the age in which we now live. The translator who mediates between the Christian context and the secular context is himself a product of the secular context and would be denying his own endowments bestowed by the Lord of creation if he divested himself of that type of equipment which comes from the secular education process in which he has shared. The critique made of the language of translators who are attempting to " carry across " the sense of the gospel into a secular environment centers upon the adequacy of their language. The criteria of adequacy will arise from two sources: the mythic structure of the gospel and the logical structure of the secular world's thought. The Christian can know what the gospel proclaims because he is participant in the community whose context is the gospel. He can discover, if he does not already know, what the secular environment says and thinks about itself. The translation must be judged equally by both criteria.

Bultmann: faith and existence. One of the boldest attempts to translate the Christian message into the twentieth century's language was begun by Rudolf Bultmann in his programmatic essay entitled " New Testament and Mythology," [70] published in the first instance in 1941. Bultmann clearly recognized that preaching required interpretation and that interpretation meant translation. The basis for testing the adequacy of Bultmann's language has already been stated. Does he translate *from* an adequate understanding of the Christian message *to* an adequate understanding of the secular environment? We are interested in this question from the viewpoint of language and to that viewpoint we confine ourselves in this critique. Put differently, has he translated the challenge of the gospel so that it can be answered or at least understood as challenge? Does his language speak *to* his hearers with the same force as the Biblical language intends?

One thing, above practically all else, must be said in Bultmann's favor: he is determined to translate the effective challenge of the gospel message. Whatever success or failure accompanies his efforts, this fact must be registered. The language that Bultmann has chosen as the vehicle for his translation is the vocabulary of the philosophy of existence. This choice, in itself, testifies to his basically correct understanding of the primacy of the category of history in any language chosen to convey the Christian message. A considerable semantic barrier is raised, however, by his choice of a German word to describe his effort. "Demythologizing," a translation of *Entmythologisierung*, may mean simply stripping away the myth, but as a more precise translation of the German word we should prefer "reversing the process of mythologizing." The term itself is quite as difficult to translate as it is to pronounce in German. If we attend closely to what Bultmann is doing, however, we shall get an operational definition of this somewhat barbarous word.

A brief and incisive section of Bultmann's essay criticizes earlier attempts to deal with the mythic element in the New Testament; through his critique of the allegorists, the older Liberals, and the History of Religions school, we are permitted a view of Bultmann's *intention*, which is in many ways clearer than the view we get from his working out of his thesis.[71] His objection to previous translations of the essence of the Christian message is that in their cavalier treatment of the mythic dimension these translators have *not* translated the eschatological feature of the gospel but have merely eliminated it. Thus Bultmann is eminently aware of the overwhelming concern of the Christian gospel with *time*. The eschatological dimension of the message cannot be preserved in a translation employing the structure of the logic of nature as its only vehicle. In so far as he maintains this stance, Bultmann is in agreement with the best modern scientific and historical thinking. Nowhere is this view more pronounced than in the process philosophy of Whitehead and his disciples. The lowest component element in process thought — the atomic event — is historical in that it is temporal and productive of novelty; this manner of thinking called the philosophy of process "is the metaphysical generalization based upon modern science." [72] The pressing question in connection with Bultmann's language is, however, whether or not it actually takes account of the full dimensions of the Christian message; that is to say, is Bultmann liable to the same charge he levels against Harnack, for instance?

Bultmann takes his cue from the Fourth Evangelist (John 5:24 f.; cf. Rom. 10:17), who succeeded, in part at least, in a translation of the eschatological act of God in Christ into an event that has ultimate significance *in the present*. For Bultmann, however, as for Luther before him, and Augustine before either, the act of God becomes significant *for me* in the acknowledgment of my creaturely status and not in my being told *about* the "authentic nature of man." [73] Here his critique of secular existentialism is most acute, for the message of the gospel tells *me* that my situation is impossible without the saving act of God; such cannot be the "message" of secular existentialism. This distinction is for Bultmann the ultimate *scandalon* of the Christian message — that in a specific human life, God has delivered us from what we can observe and describe as inauthentic existence and that apart from this historical act there is no escape from this inauthentic existence.

The decided emphasis upon the existential quality of faith and the necessity of decision in the face of an otherwise impossible situation are all to the good. It redresses the balance in a Biblical understanding of faith as trust in the same way as Luther's *sola fide* did and for precisely the same reasons. Any loss of the existential dimension of the meaning of faith amounts to an inversion of the gospel. Bultmann contends that the function of myth in the New Testament is that of expressing man's self-understanding. Since this is also what existentialism attempts, he finds justification in translating the myth into existentialist terms. To the extent that he has done this, Bultmann succeeds in the task *as he understands it*. Our difference with Bultmann arises from our view of the task incumbent upon a translator.

To begin with, Bultmann has not adequately described the function of myth in the Biblical context. The Biblical myth *does* express man's self-understanding; but it also expresses something *more*. The Biblical myth is an expression of the structure of ultimate reality. There is indeed an existential dimension of that myth which Bultmann rightly stresses, but there is a metaphysical dimension — because of Aristotelian overtones, we should perhaps avoid this term, but we prefer it — that Bultmann dismisses as merely cosmological. By limiting his understanding of myth and its function to that which is outlined by Hans Jonas,[74] Bultmann has shut the door on a fundamental aspect of the function of myth *in the Bible*. Jonas describes the function of myth in Gnosticism, but the controlling feature of the Gnostic myth, its abhorrence of history, is still present to a considerable degree in non-Christian existentialism. Bultmann has to import history into his construct as a critique of secularized existentialism before he can use this framework as a vehicle for translation. That aspect of Biblical myth which Bultmann excepts from his translation is concerned with the doctrine of creation.

In our discussion of the mythic stance of the Old Testament, we have already indicated that the Hebraic preoccupation with history issued in a mythico-historical affirmation that the God of history is the creator of the world. This concern, as we there pointed out, was not a cosmogonic concern but a metaphysical and ontological concern. Ktisiology, a term used to designate the doctrine of creation as parallel to eschatology, is fundamental to eschatology in the Biblical myth, and a sundering of eschatology from its ktisiological foundation lays eschatology open to that qualitative interpretation, by way of the Platonic phenomenal and noumenal worlds, which divorces it from its dominantly temporal characteristic. Had Bultmann been as determined to *listen* to what he calls the cosmological aspect of myth in the Biblical structure, he would have realized that *in its own terms* it gives expression to the metaphysical and ontological orientation of the Christian community; that is to say, the doctrine of creation is the Bible's expression of its reaching for an understanding of ultimate reality.

Because of a de-emphasis upon this aspect of the function of Biblical myth, Bultmann has all but cut the Christian Bible in two between the Testaments and discarded the Old Testament. In this regard, he appears to have committed the error of Marcion, an error that was perpetuated in Harnack. The only possible outcome of this procedure is a new Gnosticism. Once the ktisiological foundation of the Christian message, its expression of metaphysical and ontological concern, is sundered, the Christian myth becomes another of the savior myths of generalized Near Eastern religion. Therefore, no matter how successful Bultmann is in his translation of the mythico-historical language of the New Testament, the most he can achieve is a partial translation because he has not taken full account of the environment *from* which he translates.

This criticism of Bultmann is not made lightly, because he is an accomplished New Testament critic who should be respected for his understanding of the peculiarly mythic stance of the New Testament. Nevertheless, this criticism only emphasizes more strongly the necessity of an adequate descriptive analysis as a preliminary to historical analysis and the necessity of both before any generalized interpretation. Bultmann's conception of the Hellenistic stage of early Christian history blinds him to the equally important prior period of purely Semitic environment. In the Hellenistic stage of its history, the church had already begun to translate the doctrine of creation. Had

Bultmann taken the prologue of the Fourth Gospel as seriously as the rest of the book, he would have recognized that this Evangelist sets his proclamation in a ktisiological framework (John 1:1-3, 10) and thus asserts the priority of the metaphysical and ontological questions. Bultmann has adequately translated the *scandalon* of the gospel, but in his attempt to demythologize he does not come to terms with the question of why this event is THE *scandalon*. This problem is the core of the metaphysical question which is inseparable from the Biblical affirmation of the doctrine of creation. Eschatology and ktisiology are inseparable; hence, failure to deal with the latter truncates the view of the former.

In his translation of the semantic structure of the New Testament, Bultmann leans heavily upon the philosophical analysis of existence propounded by Martin Heidegger. His evaluation of Heidegger's analysis is nothing less than a paean of praise; he attributes to Heidegger the achievement of an almost Christian understanding outside the church.[75] However true this may be about Heidegger's *total* view, Bultmann employs only one side of that view. Heidegger is as much concerned with *Sein* (Being) as with *Dasein* (existence); therefore, he does deal with the ontological question. Heidegger's approach to the ontological problem is through the existential question, since he claims that his terms *Dasein* and *Zeitlichkeit* (temporality) are a pathway to understanding the very structure of Being.[76] Bultmann, on the other hand, seems to limit his concern to the existential problem without driving it to the ontological depths to which Heidegger does. This limitation of horizon in Bultmann's subsequent essays may account for Heidegger's hesitancy to endorse Bultmann's use of his analysis of human existence.

There is adequate reason for Bultmann's almost exclusive preoccupation with this aspect of Heidegger's thought, for this side of the problem is the one most closely connected with eschatology and Bultmann has been fascinated in his New Testament studies with the problem of eschatology. The prob-

lem of eschatology stated in Biblical terms is the problem of
the end, a temporal problem. In the terms of philosophy it is
the problem of time and finitude. Existential philosophy is so
consumingly interested in the question of time that one could
almost use this interest as a means for cataloguing a philosopher as an existentialist. Schelling and Nietzsche both escaped
from the twin traps of timelessness and the infinity of objective
time by resorting to a temporal category that resembles the
mythic category of the *eschaton*. Kierkegaard introduced the
notion of the " pregnant moment " (*Augenblick*) as that moment in which time and eternity are tangent and a decision is
demanded. To this notion he added the concept of " con-
temporaneity " (*Gleichzeitigkeit*) whereby all history could
become a present reality. Heidegger's radical distinction between objective time and existential time left no place for the
timeless and demanded that objective time be understood in
terms of experienced or existential time. This reversal of the
order of understanding permitted Bultmann to use Heidegger's
analysis of time and finitude as a vehicle for translating the
eschatological dimension of the Biblical myth.

The peculiar strength of Bultmann's translation is, however,
the strength of a sermon. No sermon ever expounds the whole
of the Christian message, but by concentration upon a text or
a single aspect of the Biblical proclamation the preacher attempts to reach his hearers and *convert* them from hearers into
participants. Not that the preacher claims that *he* does the
converting — the conversion is achieved, he would say, by the
power of the Word through the Spirit. The preacher who addresses potential believers aims to create the atmosphere in
which the conversion may take place. Whether Bultmann
would agree that his effort is primarily a guide for preachers
must remain an open question, but the group among whom he
has enjoyed the heartiest acclaim is a group of preachers. A
reading of the so-called " Bultmann debate " as it has thus far
been translated creates the impression that it is carried on
almost exclusively among scholars and professional theologians.

This impression is due, in part at least, to the absence in the English translation of an essay fully two thirds as long as Bultmann's original essay; this essay is written by a working pastor.[77] The omission of this essay may have been dictated by economy or interest; whatever may be the reason, its absence in the English translation creates a distorted image of the controversy for those who read no German.

Theologians and philosophers may debate about the aptness of Bultmann's program of demythologizing, but preachers must ascend the pulpit steps Sunday after Sunday to proclaim the living Word. For the preacher, Bultmann's program offers a a point of contact with the hearer and makes it possible for preachers to speak *to* modern man rather than merely *at* him. The eschatological dimension of the gospel, reflecting the urgency of the Israelite prophets' warnings, is the appropriate one for the *involvement* of the hearer. If it is possible, in terms he can understand, to reach the modern man for whom the mythic structure of Biblical thinking is neither expressive nor relevant, he can be brought to an apprehension of his real situation and thereby put into the way of the gospel proclamation. The question then devolves upon whether or not the existentialist categories give an adequate expression to the eschatological dimension of the gospel's proclamation. Here is precisely where Bultmann's approach is most successful, and it is a ground upon which none but the most conservative preachers would disagree with him.

The delineation of man's existential estrangement from himself and from the structure of the world in which he lives is a necessary *praeparatio evangelica*, for the decision which each man must make is not *about* whether a given natural fact took place but *for* his future. If the way in which this generation must be approached in order to make its frustrations come clear in their deepest dimensions is via the categories of existentialism, then we must use these categories to translate the urgency of the Christian proclamation. In other words, if the meaning enshrined in the eschatological myth of the Bible can be pointed to in terms of our current self-understanding, then the question, to which trust in the God and Father of our Lord Jesus Christ is the answer, must be formulated in terms of that self-understanding. This is not the only question that ought to be raised and dealt with, but it is chronologically the first that must be faced. The ontological and metaphysical questions that lie beneath this question will be faced in Christian terms only by those who have been confronted by the earlier question. Consequently, on the ground upon which Bultmann is understood among the German preachers, he raises the right questions, or more properly, creates the atmosphere in which the right questions can be understood as questions. Therefore as a kerygmatic device, the demythologizing program of Bultmann performs its task. As a *systematic theology*, it is too much concerned with only one side of the Biblical myth.

The Biblical myth makes its metaphysical and ontological thrust by way of its doctrine of creation; but, as we have already indicated, the conception of creation there delineated grows out of its historical character and is not a reflection upon the patterns of nature. If, as Ps. 19 says, "the heavens declare the glory of God," this is so because he is Yahweh. The song of praise is directed to the One already known in history who has been recognized as responsible for *all* that *happens*, including the phenomena of nature. Therefore, to preserve the logical order of the myth, the decision made upon the basis of recognition of our real position in history should produce the question to which the doctrine of creation is the answer. Since the doctrine of creation is not the answer to the question, "Who made the world?" but is rather of the order, "What is the relation to ultimate reality of the One who has met us in certain historical encounters?", the metaphysical and ontological questions thus follow upon an affirmative response to the existential question implied in the kerygma. Such an understanding places in proper perspective what appear, on the surface, to be scientifically verifiable statements about the origin of the universe.

Two further points must be observed, however, with regard to the process of translation; one of them deals with preaching and the other with theological thought — hence, one can act as summary for Bultmann and the other can introduce Tillich. The preacher speaks from inside the Christian community. While no small part of his task involves an address to that community, we are here more concerned with his address to potential believers. There is a close relation between *kērygma*, which is the content of the preaching of the church, and *paraklēsis*, which is the activity of a preacher when he is speaking to the inner community. In the activity of *paraklēsis* he is repeating what the community has heard again and again, but in his role as missionary to potential believers he is making them hearers for the first time.

From an understanding of the situation of the man outside the Christian community, the preacher is required to relate that situation in all its depth to the understanding of man's situation in gospel terms. Thus he is a translator. Yet the preacher may have to know more about the real situation of man than his hearer actually knows about his own situation. In this effort, the preacher seeks the best possible analysis of man's situation in terms of that situation itself. Here Heidegger and the other philosophers of existence have made a real contribution; they have been aided by existentialist psychoanalysis represented by such thinkers as Theodor Reik. To translate the gospel via such terms is to take advantage of a recovery of understanding regarding man's isolation from himself as a category for describing his tragic situation. To perform this translation is not to equate the gospel with existentialism or with depth psychology. It is to translate the urgency of decision represented in the Christian myth by the eschatological dimension into a *similar* category in the scientific language of man. The purpose of such preaching is to put before a man the real alternatives involved in his self-understanding. The acceptance of the Christian gospel is the acceptance of a historical act of God in Christ which is related to the real situation of a man and the alternatives open to him in his situation. The acceptance of the act of God in Christ is the acceptance of Christ, but it results in becoming a member of a unique fellowship whose meaning and purpose is the service of God in Christ's name.[78] This is only the first step in the translation, however, for it is aimed at producing the grounds upon which an authentic acceptance or rejection of Jesus as the Christ can be made in the total dimensions of reality.

Tillich and the ontological question. The second step in translation involves the stance of the church toward the structure and meaning of ultimate reality, however conceived. If the preacher aims to create the conditions under which it is possible for *a* man to affirm *that* Christ is his future, then the second step involves probing into *how* and *in what way* Christ is the future of the community of relationship into which this affirmation brings that man. From the standpoint of the Bible's mythic structure, there is no such thing as an isolated believer. Biblical anthropology (view of man) sees man as a related being, or put another way, the Biblical doctrine of the church is inseparable from the Christian proclamation. In terms of Judaism, the faith affirmation was culminated by incorporation into Israel, the *populus Dei*. In Christian terms, confession of trust in God as evidenced by acceptance of Christ was culminated in Baptism, which is initiation into a community that is continuous with the apostolic Christian church, which in turn considered itself the new covenant community re-created from a remnant of Israel, the old covenant community.

When the Christian community affirms that Christ is its future, it does so in the total context of reality and not in some isolated segment of that context. This is true because of the historical character of the Christian affirmation. By this affirmation, however, the church affirms not only that Christ is *its* future, but that he is the future of all that exists or has existed.

If he is the future of this "all," he must be its past as well. This sort of affirmation places the church in the position of having a systematic view of reality and raises the question of the relation between this systematic view and that espoused by various schools of philosophy. Because the Christian affirmation is fundamentally one of relationship, Christian faith has no built-in metaphysics. This does not mean that metaphysics is of no concern to the Christian church, but it implies that there is and must be a constant line of communication kept open between theology and philosophy.

This second step of translation is performed for the church by its systematic theologians who are concerned with the structure of reality that is delineated not only by them but by responsible philosophers as well. Thus, philosophy and theology are occupied with the same subject matter, but the difference between them is one of stance with reference to this subject matter.[79] When the systematist takes up the problems of the structure and meaning of ultimate reality, he deals with them from the viewpoint of the mythic structure of the Christian affirmation of trust in the Lord of all history including nature and from the viewpoint of the philosophic structure of reality. His purpose is to relate these views in such a way that the former is not merely set aside for the latter. The systematist is no mere describer or detached spectator, however, for he is involved in the mythic structure and translates that involvement into the philosophic language. Before he can do this, he must be able to describe accurately what the mythic structure is.

In order to translate this mythic structure into the language of philosophy, however, he must also be adequately familiar with the best description of the structure of ultimate reality in philosophic terms. This is so because he continues to pose the question: How is it possible to believe in the God whom we have met and by whom we have been met in Christ when we take full account of the description of ultimate reality made by responsible philosophical inquiry? As he strives to answer that question, the systematist is neither rigging his metaphysics nor misunderstanding the function of mythic structure in the Biblical narrative. Thus, the systematist performs the church's task for the church in a culture for which the Christian affirmation is not *integral*.

Of the attempts at translation in systematic scope that are currently available, no one can doubt the singular place occupied by Tillich's *Systematic Theology*. At the moment (1960), only two of three volumes projected have appeared, but the thrust of the system is evident. The depth to which he has probed the dogmatic-kerygmatic Christian proclamation as well as the total understanding of human existence presently offered is astounding. Systematic theology owes its present conception of the nature and scope of its task, in large measure, to Tillich's rediscovery and restatement of the dimensions of the translator's mission, and to his careful delineation of the distinctions in function among the various branches of theological study.[80]

As a systematist, Tillich also examines with great care the systems of the past pointing out their success both in determining what questions are implied in human existence and what answers to these questions are implied in divine revelation. As he contrasts his own system both with past systems and with current alternatives, he demonstrates how his own method of " correlation " is a creative contribution to the translation of the Christian message into the language of our day. The essential point in his method is the recognition that the superficial questions of human existence are not directly answered by an equally superficial set of answers gleaned from the Biblical and theological field. Thus, as Tillich approaches his task, he is intent upon analyzing human existence to discover the questions it poses and to penetrate the traditional symbols used by the Christian church to expose them to the questions implied in human existence.

As Tillich outlines his approach in preliminary discussion,

it is similar to what we have tried to show as the translator's approach. In our exposition, the logic of the Biblical myth is such that it precludes translation without remainder into a language governed by the logic of nature. If this had never before been realized — and we have tried to show that it has — it would certainly become apparent to anyone who took the trouble to listen to what is being said by the philosophy of linguistic analysis. Yet, there is a real question of language, and therefore of logic, that is raised by Tillich's selection of a basic category for translating the Biblical myth. When he uses "New Being" to characterize that "reality in which the self-estrangement of our existence is overcome, a reality of reconciliation and reunion, of creativity, meaning, and hope," [81] has Tillich employed the best language available? While Being may be the ultimate category in the philosophic structure to which he is making his "reply" in the name of Christian faith, is this category an adequate vehicle for translating the Biblical myth's concern with creativity?

The total impression one gains from Tillich's system, in its present state of completion, is that he is bound to and critical of the entire Western ontological inquiry. And he is both at once! His criticism of Western ontology is much more apparent, however, than his bondage to it. In his criticism of the method used in previous ontological inquiry, Tillich reminds us us of no one more than Heidegger. Yet, he reflects the same philosophical avoidance of the place of nature which is adumbrated in Heidegger, if not actually expressed. This fact is evident in his choice of Being as his basic and irreducible category. He is far from unaware of the difficulty involved in this choice of a basic term, for he is quick to point out that it is in the concrete person of Jesus as the Christ that we meet (and are met by?) the "New Being". Hence the adjective is quite as important as the noun, and the whole term is not intended as an abstraction. Recognizing that oversimplification often results in distortion, we should still wish to press farther the question of whether Being does justice to the richness of the core of the creation-eschatology myth in which the Biblical message is cast.

In order to point out the dimensions of the question in fuller clarity, we must restate, in outline at least, the internal structure of the Biblical myth as it pertains to ontology. The God of Israel, Yahweh, has acted eschatologically in and through Jesus the Christ in such a way as to assert his sovereignty over the entire world in all its totality. This world includes the total realm of experience. While this act is *new* and *creative*, it is at the same time revelatory of the end and consistent with the beginning. By participation in this act of God, which means incorporation into the church, the believer is not delivered *from* ambiguity (the sinful structure of a fallen world) but is enabled to overcome ambiguity. The tension of sin and freedom is quite as much present in the new community of relationship with God who is the source of freedom as it was in the former context of broken relationship (both with reference to self and the rest of reality including God). But in Christ who is the " new creation " the depth of life's ambiguities is revealed and transcendence of those ambiguities is made possible because they are met and *lived through.*

Thus, the arena in which life's choices are met and lived through is the ever-changing but ever-present *now.* This " now " is inherently related to every past " now " that has been unique in the structure of its possibilities, but this " now " is also the product of the past " now's " by way of emergence. Each of these " now's " can be unfolded to reveal inside it a previous structure until this process finally yields the " now " of creation, before which there is apparently nothing. That is to say, if the chain *could* be unstrung, the ultimate point is creation, itself the act of God. Another way of saying this is that as long as there has been a world, there has been the God who creates. On the other side of this " now," there is also a chain of " now's " which ends in an act of God which is as decisive as creation. The nature of that act is revealed in the act of God in Christ who is at the same time the new act or the "new creation."

Yet, an inescapable and necessary ingredient of the myth is the saved and saving community which is *consciously* the object of the forgiveness of God for its failures to achieve the perfection of forgiveness which is its only proper response to the forgiveness of God. This community can achieve that perfection only in the arena of relations among its members and toward the rest of the world. The normative relation of that community to nature is determined by its acknowledgment that God created it, while its normative relation toward other human beings is further determined by its owning the fact that in Christ forgiveness and reconciliation have been effected in a way that is consistent both with God's primary act and his ultimate act.

Now, when Tillich speaks of Jesus Christ as the "New Being," he *seems* to have translated the "God who acts" of the creation-eschatology myth into the "God who is" of idealist philosophy. Thereby Tillich appears to escape the temporal category together with all the problems inherent in what is meant by God's creativity. One of the problems that is either escaped or touched only by implication is in what way or to what extent God precedes the temporal process. The other side of this problem is whether and in what way God or man either survives or overcomes the temporal process together with its ambiguities. In moving from the basic ground of creativity, which is the ontological ground of the myth, to Being, Tillich seems to have admitted the very duality he is determined to exclude. That is to say, he has introduced the distinction between time and eternity which underlies the structure of Western ontology from the days of Plato onward. He has made every effort to escape the static quality of Being which inheres in the systematic development of Being as a prime category, but he still appears to preserve the timelessness of Being by clinging to the changelessness of God. Yet, if God is intricately involved in the creative process, as the Biblical myth insists, how can he avoid being affected by the creative process? This is not a problem which the Biblical myth solves to complete satisfaction, but it is not avoided in the Biblical myth either. The question that keeps coming to the fore is whether or not the category of creativity is not more basic to the Biblical myth than Tillich seems to indicate in his system; if so, is this not a flaw within this vastly helpful and cogent system?

One of the difficulties that accompanied the translation of the mythic structure of the Christian proclamation into Platonic and Neoplatonic terms was the alteration suffered by the Biblical myth because Platonism had no room for a God so inextricably involved in the process of creativity. This difficulty was only partially overcome by the radical alteration of the character of the Demiurge and his function to accommodate the creator-God of the Old Testament and identify him with the God of the Platonic system. Because Platonism was built upon its own mythic conception of the world, it could not easily be transformed to accommodate another mythic structure since the Platonic myth had a semantic structure of its own. Hence the God who inhabited the eternal world of Plato was hardly equipped to play the role of the God who was intimately related to the temporal world by way of creativity and constantly involved therein by way of history. The problems encountered by Philo are a testimony to the difficulty before the Christian gospel ever began to make use of Platonism. The incompatibility of the Platonic structure and the Biblical structure was only bridged by the conciliar definitions which did not solve the problem but only kept the questions in the foreground where they belonged.

When the Aristotelian structure replaced Platonism as the vehicle for translation, it was no better able to overcome the incompatibility despite the fact that the category of causality was employed to explicate the character of God as creativity. Aristotle's Prime Mover was quite as remote from the God of Abraham, Isaac, and Jacob as he was from the process of which he was first cause. Even if he was also final cause, this made him but a dim reflection of the God who acts in creation and in the *eschaton*. Here, too, creativity had been subordinated to Being, and the heroic effort of Thomas Aquinas could not bridge the gap between Yahweh and the Prime Mover.

In spite of Tillich's defense of his use of the concept of Being,[82] it appears that certain aspects of the critique of Platonism and Aristotelianism are equally valid as a critique of the philosophy of being that underlies Tillich's system. At the same time, it is the virtue of Tillich's system that it invites such criticism. In his transformation of the Biblical metaphysic of creativity into an ontology of being, Tillich admits his association with the entire stream of Christian thought, but he seems to close the door against a metaphysic of creativity by confining the alternatives to nominalistic philosophy and personalistic theology. In accordance with his own method of correlation, it would appear that he could have kept the door open for a metaphysical structure in which time and creativity were of more importance than they seem to be in his systematic exposition.

The root of the theological use of Being as the basic concept is apparently embedded in the religious need for a transcendent God. But divine transcendence cannot be equated with spatial or temporal independence. The transcendence of God consists, we ought to say, in his creative freedom; this is another way of saying that he is not conditioned, *as we are*, by the laws governing his creation. The God of Israel who is met in Christ is really *new*, but at the same time he is not discontinuous with the God of the exodus or the God of the restoration from exile. Now, Tillich surely strives to maintain the tension between the new and the old in the nature of God, but he *tends* to reduce the new to an aspect of the old by his subjection of creativity to Being. Nels Ferré has detected this difficulty of starting with Being, for in it he sees the portal through which all the problems of Aristotle's *Actus Purus* are permitted an entry into Tillich's system.[83] The difficulty of equating God with Being-itself is underlined when we recognize that the core of the problem lies in the meaning of the terms transcendence and immanence when applied to God. Although he uses the terms, Tillich is careful to point out that they are primarily spatial symbols. So, if the question of God's relation to the world be *asked* in these terms, it is not only difficult to answer, but any answer using these particular terms would be utterly meaningless.[84] In terms of our present conception of the natural world, Tillich is surely right to reject any answer to the question that uses these terms.

Transcendence is a term that is at home in the vocabulary of theology only to the extent that it offers a corrective to a tendency toward equating God with nature. In other words, transcendence has meaning only in connection with a certain philosophical-theological system. When the distinction between transcendence and immanence is pressed to an absolute, it produces a God who is transcendental and nonnatural. The result of this sort of thinking is deism. If the terminology of transcendence and immanence is to be employed, then it will have to be redefined. Transcendence will then have to be understood in the way in which the cultural anthropologist or the social psychologist uses the word. As such it is a quality of existence which permits persons to view themselves objectively. Thus, when applied to God, it will not produce the transcendentalism which has been the bane of theologies based upon idealistic categories.

The problems encountered in Tillich's translation are only the more clearly underlined by what he explicitly denies. When he denies the classical meaning of being-itself by asserting that being-itself is a depth within beings, he effectively avoids any transcendentalism; this brings him close to *process* theologians. Yet when he denies that experience is a source of revelation, but asserts that it is a medium only, he appears to take back the classical view by granting a self-sufficiency to God as outside the process of nature and history. This self-sufficiency of God that cannot be located either inside or outside the structure of experience is further complicated by Tillich's insistence that finitude is not in itself evil, although his use of the terms "existence" and "essence" in connection with man as well as God seems to force the conclusion that finitude is equivalent to evil in the case of man. Thus it would appear that his reliance upon a philosophy of being has forced him into a series of unresolved problems, the most important of which relate to the metaphysical role played by the doctrine of creation in the Biblical myth.

Thus envisaged, Tillich's translation has some of the same strictures that apply to Bultmann's. The main difference stems from the fact that Tillich seems to be attempting more than Bultmann and therefore must be held more accountable for the shortcomings. In the end, neither Bultmann nor Tillich seems to be able to avoid the category of eternity as opposed to time; to this extent, the myth of the beginning and the end, the creation-eschatology myth, is truncated and forced into an alien structure. Tillich, particularly, cannot seem to evade the idealistic categories which so deeply underlie his system; this must be admitted, despite the brilliance and complexity of the most competent systematic theologian to have produced a system in our day.

Another alternative. We should be most shortsighted, were we not to point out that another direction is being struck in our day and in our own national scene. In spite of the critique offered of Tillich as a representative of the classical tradition philosophically, his system has the breadth and depth of Augustine. His thinking is no less catholic than that of the architect of *nostra philosophia,* but it is subject to the same restrictions. As critical of Platonism and as ready to incorporate the insights of Christian faith to modify Platonism, Tillich has caught and combined the existential thrust of the Christian proclamation with the concern for ontology that is the legacy of the Academy to Western thought. The most searching criticism of Tillich's system comes both directly and indirectly from the side of process philosophy, which is itself no less the product of that catholic inclusiveness so characteristic of Tillich. The reason for the critique must be located in the *archai*, in the *principia*, those basic principles which, in Augustine's case for example, were modified when he brought the Christian concern with history and personality to bear on the Neoplatonism of his day.

The theological viewpoint that arises from the attempt to translate the mythic Biblical structure into terms of process philosophy is no less relevant than Tillich's system. It has the added virtue of a holistic view of nature and history as intimately related, and an uncanny sensitivity to the philosophical implications of creativity. As yet, there has appeared no total systematic undertaking bearing the mark of this school of thought, but the names of Bernard Meland,[85] Bernard Loomer,[86] and Daniel Day Williams [87] will be closely associated with any systematic view that emerges from this school. The flow of philosophical thought, since the seventeenth century, has been from Europe to America; Tillich represents the finest and most recent product of that tradition which has come from Greece through Germany. On the other hand, the empiricism that has undergirded the American philosophical attitude has begun to make a real contribution to the total philosophical picture. Science, once cast in the role of religion's most virile enemy, has achieved, in its maturity, a greater sense of responsibility. Now it is in a position to make its own peculiar contribution to a positive and creative world outlook.

As a metaphysic derived from scientific description of the world, process philosophy is unique in that it is able to take into account both history and nature without reducing history to nature. The concept that made this possible was derived from post-Darwinian development of the theory of evolution as that idea was illuminated from the physical sciences. The use of the concept of " emergence " makes it possible in terms of process philosophy to deal with the unique as well as the recurrent since this concept takes account of both continuity and discontinuity. The emergent becomes the expression of creativity. The nature of God is discernible, in effect, in both nature and history. Apart from the process it is impossible to conceive God because he is given with the process as the one whose primordial nature exemplifies as well as establishes the categories and conditions of creativity. Thus, while God is religiously and ethically transcendent, a process theology would not conceive of a God who is metaphysically and epistemologically transcendent. If there is any of the latter kind of transcendence, it must be derived from the former. This is surely close to the Biblical myth since nature and history are seen as the arena of God's activity.[88]

Just as the Biblical myth can see an end as a counterpart to a beginning, so the principle of entropy which is derived from the second law of thermodynamics provides an end beyond which the emergent activity of process is inoperative. How far in the future this may be is a matter of speculation. The same is true of the interference with this process by negentropy (negative entropy) which is an unpredictable emergent. What is really important for our subject is that in the structure of reality there is revealed a leveling effect that is concomitant with the upward progress and acts as a brake upon it. Thus process philosophy in its promise of a future is aware of a point beyond which progress and emergence is no longer active. Yet the other characteristics of this systematic view of the world are likewise meaningful as a structural semantic for the communication of the Biblical myth. The social nature of reality, for instance, is an obvious outcome of an appreciation of the ongoing life of the world, for in the confluence of events there is an inescapable dimension of sociality. This is expanded onto the level of human experience wherein we come to know that we cannot realize ourselves without others being realized, for they are realized in us and we in them. How very much more comprehensible this becomes when we translate into these terms the notion of forgiveness, for we know that we cannot be realized unless we *are* forgiven, no matter how penitent we may be.

What all this comes to is the metaphysical immanence of

God, which is perhaps better expressed as the transparence of God through his activity, together with a transcendence that is religious and ethical. This means to say, of course, that God cannot achieve self-realization apart from his creatures; and thus, the forgiveness of God, which is his mercy, is a part of the process in which the nature of God is revealed in the restoration of broken relationship. But this forgiveness of God is likewise an inexorable judgment because we turn from it and refuse it only to deny what we experience even in our own imperfect relations with one another.

We can do no more than point to this direction of thought. It is far from systematized at this point, but the leads it has taken are exciting and challenging. It is still a question as to whether or not this direction of thought will be able to deal with the redemptive quality of God's activity, but already this seems to present a problem. Perhaps, the most fruitful line of endeavor will combine the eschatological insight of an existentialist theology with the ktisilogical insight of process theology. If this comes to pass, a new emergent will appear in theological communication which will answer the criticisms we have directed toward each of the systematic expositions examined herein.

Chapter VI

Toward a Language
for Responsible Communication

As this study has developed, we have attempted to make it
clear that any language employed by the church for the communication of its gospel to the world is purely instrumental.
A language used for this purpose is what we mean by theological language. It acts as a communicative bridge between the
religious ethos and a *secular* environment. If a theological language has performed its task adequately in a given period, it
will become outmoded in time and need replacement. How
drastically the theological language will have to be revised
depends to a large extent upon how much different the outlook
of the newer environment is from that of the former. We have
also tried to point out some of the reasons for the fluidity of
theological language. These reasons tend to focus upon the
semantic structure of the Christian affirmation and its essential
distinction from that of other viewpoints. The dimensions of
the present task of developing a viable theological language
are to be measured by the semantic structure of Christian
thought, as we can understand it at the moment, and by the
semantic structure of the culture with which we are attempting
to establish communication. The task is both complicated and
simplified by the fact that some sort of communication has
been going on between the church's viewpoint and Western
culture since before the emergence of the Christian church
from Judaism. Whether this history is bane or blessing depends
upon how we study and understand it *as history.*

In one sense, of course, the pole, which is created by the religious language of the church and to which our theological language must be anchored, remains unalterable. Our *view* of this pole may and does change, however, by virtue of a deepening and broadening apprehension of the semantic structure of the religious language. The Bible unites the church with its own past, and this is what is meant by characterizing the Bible as normative for Christian faith. This normative literature, witnessing those events in response to which the church came into existence, is not *merely* literature. The church treats the Bible as normative in its totality; yet, it is employed not as a reference book but within a liturgical context. That is to say, the church uses the Bible in a peculiar way as the recitation of its *raison d'être*. The use of the Bible in the liturgical worship of the church is in accordance with a calendaric cycle that provides the context, and in this context the events constitutive of the church's existence as they are narrated in the Bible are relived in remembrance. The calendaric framework has a weekly dimension as well as an annual dimension both of which were inherited from the Jewish community in which the church came into existence.

The weekly observance of the Jewish community on the Sabbath Day is oriented toward creation. The Jews celebrated the total act of God's creation on the seventh day, the Sabbath, whereon God rested from his good work (Gen. 1:31 to 2:3). From a very early point in its history, the Christian church remembered thankfully before God on the first day of the week, Sunday, the Lord's Day (*kuriakē*, Greek; *dominica*, Latin), the event from which *its* existence was to be dated — God's raising Jesus from the dead. This thanksgiving (*eucharistia*) to the God of Israel, Yahweh, at first probably existed alongside of, but eventually replaced, the synagogue observance on the Sabbath. On the first day of the week each week the Christians remembered the newly creative act of God in the raising of Jesus. This act was paralleled by God's first act of creation (Gen. 1:3-5), but it was a culmination or fulfillment of that act in a new act. The first day of the week was for Christians, therefore, the eighth day of the old week and signified the new beginning or new creation by God after the old had passed away. The Eastern Church has assimilated its weekly and annual calendars so that the emphasis upon the raising of Jesus as the creative act of God is carried to its logical conclusion; the church year begins in that part of the church on Easter Day.

The annual calendar of Judaism beginning with Passover was oriented toward deliverance. Passover celebrated the deliverance from oppression in Egypt, and Pentecost was related to the giving of the Torah at Sinai. In its annual cycle of remembrance and observance, the Christian church also took up this theme and related the act of God in Christ to the great deliverance from Egypt. In its earliest stages of development, the Christian liturgical year was hardly distinguishable from the Jewish annual cycle. It began with Passover, which celebrated the raising of Jesus as a new exodus whereby a new *populus Dei* was created out of the old. The first addition to the Christian calendar was Pentecost (*shevuoth*), the Feast of Weeks, and in the early Christian calendar it marked the close of the fifty-day period of annual rejoicing over the new exodus. In time, this feast was reinterpreted so that it achieved a newer but deeper sense of the end of the rejoicing. As Acts, ch. 2, reflects, it became the point at which the church commemorated its venture forth as a missionary church. As the Christian calendar developed a character of its own, it began to expand. The events of Jesus' life leading up to the raising from the dead were commemorated prior to Passover, thus giving us the Lenten season, and the events constitutive of the church's understanding of its beginning were worked out in greater detail and attached to the days between Passover and Pentecost. Much of this development took place after the church had left Jewish ground, but the Passover-Pentecost annual cycle as well as the weekly cycle had been fixed at an early date. Thus the calendar enshrined the structural seman-

tic of the myth and acted to reinforce the Biblical structure in
the life of the church.

The further development of the Christian annual calendar
took shape in the Hellenistic world and derived its dating from
the culture in which the church found its new home. The
Jewish annual cycle, taken into the Christian calendar with
new meaning, was lunar in computation. The new feast cycle
including Christmas and Epiphany represented a series of
pagan feasts of fixed date, computed on a solar basis, taken into
the calendar and invested with a meaning derived from certain
aspects of the *life* of Jesus. Thus the developed Christian annual calendar exhibits both a solar cycle and a lunar cycle.
This accounts for the elasticity of the end of the Epiphany
season, which is calculated on the solar basis, and the end of
the Pentecost (Trinity) season, which is calculated on the
lunar basis, for each year the solar and lunar cycles must be
adjusted to each other.

The point about this combined calendar, consisting of a
weekly observance and an annual observance, which is itself
a fusion of two stages of development, is that this is the framework in which the church reads and knows its normative literature. This reliving of constitutive events in thankful remembrance, or Eucharistic anamnesis, puts against the total cycle
of events as background the specific event being commemorated at any point in the church's year. Thus when we speak
of the Bible and its language as being normative for the
church, it is implied that the church's affirmation of faith is
reiterated in this liturgical framework. The total framework
constitutes the semantic structure of the church's *religious* language. Thus, if we are to appreciate the dimension of Christian religious language, we must take into account that
Scripture and liturgy exist in a dynamic union within the community's life, forming its fabric of meaning. Scripture is read
and understood in liturgical worship, and liturgy interprets
Scripture. Both together constitute the environment in which
the Christian church understands itself as the object of God's

redemptive love in Christ and the instrument whereby that redemptive love is shed abroad in the rest of creation.

On the other side of the polar situation in which Christian
communication operates is to be found the secular world,
which is far from a unity. Into the various structures that make
up this secular world the Christian community attempts to
translate its gospel message in order that it may be heard.
Seizing wherever he can upon categories that are useful, the
theologian tries to create that situation in the secular thought
world which will make the church's religious affirmation understandable. This process of establishing and enlarging communication with the world outside the church is a reciprocal
process if the theologian is responsible and maintains integrity.
His own insights must be subjected to the same scrutiny as that
to which he would subject those of the world with which he
seeks a fruitful communicative interchange. In other words,
his faith affirmation must be related to truth; in humility he
will know that the truth is one and that he cannot possess truth
in its entirety. Therefore, *theological* language is always a
function of two factors: (1) the semantic structure of the
church's religious affirmation as it is most responsibly understood and (2) the semantic structure of the world addressed
by the church. The theologian's language thus reflects the
bifocal view of the church *for* whom he speaks and the world
to whom he speaks.

At the outset, the Christian church was able to set up a line
of communication with the alien Hellenistic world because the
language which bound that world together was turned to the
church's use by its preachers as well as its budding theologians.
Translating the gospel into the *koinē* Greek that was the traffic
language of the Hellenistic world was superficially a simple
task, because this language had been prepared in part by the
translation of the Old Testament and by some Jewish literature
of a communicative nature. It was an especially easy task for
members of the second Christian generation like Paul, and it
remained so for later generations. The reason for this was that

Paul and his contemporaries were basically oriented toward Judaism. In the generations that succeeded, however, the risk involved in the translation of the gospel increased in proportion to the predominance in the church of Gentiles, that is, Greek Christians.

In the earliest generations, the semantic structure of the theological language employed was almost exclusively Semitic and mythic. None of the great Hellenistic Jewish interpreters of Israelite religion became Christians, with the result that the early Christians in the Hellenistic Church had to depend largely upon pedestrian minds to whom the Hellenistic world view was hardly even known. Even Paul, who was thoroughly at home in the Hellenistic Greek of his day, was not deeply aware of the structure of Hellenistic thought. Although he was capable of exploiting to the fullest the Hellenistic rhetoric practiced in the mid-first century, he was not governed by the structural semantic of Hellenistic Greek. Paul was a Jew, and his religious orientation, Jewish first and then Christian, structured his thinking in such a way that it has become almost a tradition that he was bilingual. The evidence for his having had more than the most rudimentary familiarity with any Semitic language is nonexistent, but the persistence of the tradition is a testimony to his lack of any real orientation toward Greek thinking.

Paul and his contemporaries formed a bridge to the Hellenistic world. They were familiar enough with Aramaic to carry on negotiations with the apostolic generation, probably without the aid of professional interpreters, but the communication was possible because they shared so fully the orientation of that company. They knew Greek because it was their native tongue and the tongue in which they had acquired their knowledge of the Judaism in which they had been reared and out of which they had come. For that combination of reasons, they preached and wrote a Semitically oriented gospel in a language to which, linguistically at least, it was not altogether foreign because of the Septuagint.

It is doubtful, however, whether the church could have advanced beyond the sect stage if each succeeding generation had been of the same general sort as Paul's generation. The post-Pauline literature, represented by such divergent strains as James, the Pastorals, First Peter, Hebrews, and even the Fourth Gospel, all reflects a significant alteration in stance. There is enough more of Hellenism in each of these works to demonstrate how much closer to Hellenism their authors stood than did Paul. Each of them exhibits a slightly greater involvement in the Hellenistic thought world than Paul, but that slight increment set a pattern that is discernible in succeeding generations. It is not until well into the second century that the distinction emerges clearly, but a backward glance from that point reveals a slowly but surely developing pattern. The gospel had begun to feel more at home in the Greek world.

As the second century yielded to the third and the third to the fourth, not only Greek but also Latin would become the language of the church and provide more and more of the structure in which its thinking would take place. Already in the second century, but much more noticeably in the third and fourth, the caliber of mind represented by the Christian thinker improved because the church was successfully attracting men of high stature intellectually — look, for instance, at Clement, Origen, Athanasius, and Augustine. These men were not Jews, and in most respects they were incapable of thinking like Paul or his immediate successors. They were Greeks in language, but so was Paul. Much more importantly, the semantic structure in which they thought was Hellenistic, and this was not the case with Paul. The intellectual equipment that these men brought to the Christian cause was both an advantage and a disadvantage, but without them the church would have stagnated.

On the one hand, it was a blessing that the church was able to attract that whole succession of men whom we know as the Greek and Latin fathers. The greater of these men forced their Christian affirmation to the very limits of what they understood as truth. They could not withdraw from the world in which they had once lived, nor could they divest themselves of their former impetus to search for the fullest implications of their premises. Their inclination was to go back into that world which had nourished them, and armed with the gospel to convince that world of the way in which the gospel both judged and illumined what that world knew and was seeking. The conversion of these intellectuals produced a literature so marked by its catholic inclusiveness that it assumed a position something like a second line of defense approaching, in its normative aspects, the first line represented by the Scriptures and the liturgy.

These men made it possible for the church to *think* in Greek and eventually in Latin. Consequently, the church could not only *present* its gospel to the pagan world, but it could also *defend* that gospel in open conflict with the pagan world's best thinkers. As an outstanding example of this process, one need only read the *Contra Celsum* of Origen,[89] which is virtually unrivaled by anything produced in the secular world during the third century. Of this aspect of the achievement of the Greek and Latin fathers, it is hardly possible to speak too glowingly. A risk was involved, it is true, as is demonstrated by the various systems against which the church had to pronounce. Nevertheless, this was a small price to pay for the gains registered by the church in communicating with the pagan world.

On the other hand, however, the negative aspects must be noted as well. Although it was enshrined in the liturgy whose resistance to radical change preserved at least the form of it, that particular orientation to time which is inseparable from eschatology was lost by the church during this period. The eschatological dimension of the historic Eucharistic liturgy could not be irretrievably lost because of its structure, but the language in which this dimension was couched could be reinterpreted in terms of a structure differing markedly from the Biblical myth. Gradually but certainly the Greek myth of generality — the myth of two worlds, one eternal and the other temporal — supplanted the Hebraic myth of the end. With the triumph of the Greek structure of reality, the Hebraic emphasis upon time as a basic category yielded to Greek spatial thinking, and the eschatological structure was interpreted qualitatively. The concept of the church as the eschatological *populus Dei* gave way to the myth of the " here and the hereafter " with emphasis upon the " hereafter " as the real and the consequent devaluation of the " here " as but a shadow. The immortality of the soul replaced resurrection as the content of the Christian hope. Hebraic corporeity was turned into classical individualism. The transformation of the Christian outlook by these subtle changes resulted in making Christianity an otherworldly religion. The change was not abrupt, but a glance at the Latin Church of, say, the tenth century shows the magnitude of the transformation. By that time, the church was saving *souls out of* the world, while the proclamation that " God was in Christ reconciling the world to himself " (II Cor. 5:19) had been turned inside out. The church as a corporate entity that acted as the locus of the Spirit's operation for the redemption of the whole created order had been lost to mind as well as to sight. There is no specific point at which we could confidently say that this change took place, but the fact of the change is incontrovertible. Dionysius the Areopagite had achieved a delayed victory over another earlier contender at the Areopagus.

The reason for the change is not hard to trace. Once the church had learned to think in classical categories, it was difficult, if not impossible, for men of lesser stature than Athanasius and Augustine to prevent these categories from achieving dominance as the semantic structure in which their thought took place. As a result of the profound contribution of the Greek fathers, even the Bible was read and studied through the eyes of classical thought. It was but a step to interpreting the Scriptures by way of that thought structure. In effect, the church had canonized the Scriptures as normative and preserved the liturgical context in which they were understood as normative, but the actual norm was to be found in the mediated classicism that permeated Western culture.

One of the most important aspects of the Reformation was the recapturing of the normative character of the Bible. The early Reformers performed a singular service to communication of the gospel when they made this break through the classical norm. Luther and Calvin both contributed mightily to breaking the hold of the classical Greco-Roman semantic structure upon the mind of the church. The failure of the Reformation in this respect was due to the successors of the Reformers who were incapable of carrying out the revolution in semantic structure that was inherent in the challenges of both Calvin and Luther. The ecclesiastical polity and the liturgical structure that characterized the post-Reformation Protestant and Reformed Churches were a reflection of their theological orientation. Together these aspects of post-Reformation Christianity showed that Protestant and Reformed Churches alike only dimly perceived the depth to which Luther and Calvin had shaken the edifice of Western Christendom. The same general critique of the later Reform movements could also be made; leaders like Wesley are venerated but hardly understood in the traditions that claim these leaders as founders or reformers. As the theology and the church life of the Reformation Churches developed, it became obvious that they were not able to rescue the church's thought from its slavery to the semantic structure of classicism. They were captive, in effect, to the same viewpoint as that which crystallized post-Tridentine Roman Catholicism into as rigid a sect as any other in Christendom.

As we face the task of communicating responsibly with what has been variously described as a post-Christian world, we cannot afford any longer to carry the excess baggage of an outmoded theological language. This generation must break through the chains that bind us to the semantic structure of classicism, or else we shall forfeit our chance to speak to the world. Too much translation of the message of the gospel has been secondhand translation. We cannot take as normative the thirteenth, the ninth, the fifth, or even the third century. A translation of the gospel using any of these levels as normative is as pointless as using an English translation of the Vulgate as the Biblical text for a translation of the Bible into Telugu. In the missionary activity of the church and in the experience of the younger churches, it is becoming evident that it is unnecessary to make Platonists, Aristotelians, or children of the Enlightenment out of non-Western peoples before they can hear the Christian message and understand it as well as we do. Those churches which are aware of this fact are making a concerted effort to put the theological language of the church on a sound footing in cultures that have never even had more than unfortunate contact with the Western world. The corollary of this fact has not been as clearly recognized by the church with reference to its task in the twentieth-century Western world.

The main reason for failure to appreciate that the classical structure was instrumental and not absolute is a misunderstanding of the real value of the traditional theological thought of Western Christendom. The history of Christian thought is studied in depth in order to appreciate how, under given circumstances, the church has thought about certain aspects of its proclamation. This study is illuminative and directive; it is exemplary of a method of translation. It is not normative in content, however; there is only one normative literature, and that is Scripture. There is nothing indispensable about the Greek structuring of the Christian proclamation during the first half-dozen centuries of the church's life. Translators of the church's message must not only study the translation, however, for they must know the structure of the world to which this translation was addressed if they are to understand it as a translation. Translators study this phase of the translation process in order to acquire an approach to translation. Their interest is in appreciating the method and approach and not in repeating the content of the translation.

The ante-Nicene church was successful in forging a language for Christian communication with the Hellenistic world be-

cause that church *translated* its religious language into a theological language employing the semantic structure of the Greek
philosophical vocabulary. Theirs was a bold venture since
Judaism offered only abortive precedents. Since there was no
working model on which they could pattern their undertaking,
the church fathers had to be innovators. In an important sense,
these early Christian communicators were charting seas previously untraveled. As we follow in their footsteps, we should
be well advised to use their charts for no more than what they
really are. Studying their charts will help us materially to understand how charts are made, but the charts we have to make
must provide as accurate a description of the seas we intend
to sail as theirs were of the waters over which they had to
travel.

At this point in our cultural history, we have adequate tools
for devising a language effective for Christian communication
to our contemporaries. We are aware of the dimensions of the
semantic structure of the mythic form of expression in which
Christian religious language is cast. We have been made increasingly conscious of the structure that underlies the Hellenistic view of the world and of the way in which this view was
modified by the outstanding theologians of the Greek and
Latin Churches to convey, however altered, the Christian
conception of man and the world. A good beginning has been
made toward a responsible conception of the world as it is
delineated by modern scientific research in all of its manifold
aspects. The inference to be drawn from these insights is that
a translation of the Christian message from the mythic context
of Christian religious language to a language accessible to
modern man need not pass through the "halfway house" of
Hellenism. We cannot avoid philosophy when we translate the
Christian gospel, but this does not mean that we must understand "philosophy" as the equivalent of "Greek philosophy."

The language to be employed for Christian communication
in our day must be at least as effective as that employed in
previous eras. If it is to be effective for Christian *communica-*

tion, it will have to reflect all of human knowledge and experience including that of the scientific era in which we now live. If it is to be effective for *Christian* communication, it will have to reflect the peculiarly Christian myth as we now understand it. As we have surveyed the current scene, we have seen how deeply our era is concerned in one way or another with all the problems inherent in achieving a total view of the world. Linguistic science, the philosophy of linguistic analysis, and the philosophy of symbolic form are deepening our understanding of what language does and how it works. Aided on the scientific level by various psychological studies of the unconscious and by clinical research of psychiatrists, the philosophers of existence are probing for a yet more comprehensive conception of what it means to be or to exist. Correspondingly, an existentially oriented social psychology, reflected in certain expressions of the philosophy of existence, is making us profoundly cognizant of our inevitable involvement with one another with the result that we begin to perceive how utterly frustrating must be any attempt to understand human personality atomistically and individualistically — man is at least a social being, if he is man at all.

The philosophers of process are drawing together and making generalizations from the observations of half a hundred independent fields of scientific inquiry. Their constructive view of ultimate reality has restored to metaphysics a dynamic that Christian thought cannot but welcome. Each of these fields of study has its own peculiar structure that provides its semantic. No one of these structures is adequate by itself to serve uncriticized as the vehicle for translation of the Christian message. Each can make its contribution to the Christian enterprise of translation, however, when we understand that each of these fields of inquiry is like a band of colored light in the spectrum of truth that is refracted through experience.

If we shall take seriously the task of translation, the language of translation will emerge. Translation is a dynamic function, however, which consists of relating two structures each of which has previously been adequately understood on its own terms by the translator. The impetuous translator who attempts to avoid or truncate the preparatory steps involved in acquiring adequate familiarity with both structures will produce a translation that does injustice to one or both of the structures involved.

The conception of translation that we have advocated in this study is derived scientifically from linguistic science. It is completely compatible, however, with our understanding of the Christian gospel. As God in Christ entered concretely into a specific culture at a given time and place, so the message of his revelatory-redemptive act must become incarnate in and for each generation by entering the culture of that generation and redeeming it. This is the task of the church as it seeks to share this unique and unrepeatable act of God with the world which he created and which he redeemed by this new act of creation in Christ whereby he also finally revealed himself.

Notes

1. For the clearest exposition of this problem known to the author, see C. N. Cochrane, *Christianity and Classical Culture* (Clarendon Press, Oxford, 1940), pp. 232 ff., 359–398. Appreciation of this problem is basic to an understanding of the real points at issue in the struggles over Christology in the fourth and fifth centuries.

2. "*Quid ergo Athenis et Hierosolymis? quid academiae et ecclesiae? quid haereticis et christianis?*" Tertullian, *De praescriptione haereticorum* vii. 9 (translation my own).

3. *Logos* is used by the Fourth Evangelist with reference to Jesus as *Logos* of God only in the Prologue; "Son" does not appear in the Prologue (cf. John 1:34, 42).

4. Otto Neurath (ed.), *International Encyclopedia of Unified Science* (University of Chicago Press, 1938–   ).

5. John Wilson, *Language and the Pursuit of Truth* (Cambridge University Press, Cambridge, 1956).

6. Wilson, *Language and Christian Belief* (St. Martin's Press, Inc., 1958).

7. Ian T. Ramsey, *Religious Language: An Empirical Placing of Theological Phrases* (S.C.M. Press, Ltd., London, 1957).

8. Ben F. Kimpel, *Language and Religion: A Semantic Preface to a Philosophy of Religion* (Philosophical Library, Inc., 1957).

9. Basil Mitchell (ed.), *Faith and Logic: Oxford Essays in Philosophical Theology* (George Allen & Unwin, Ltd., London, 1957). As further evidence of the impact of this philosophical trend in British thought, we may cite also Anthony Flew and Alasdair Mac-

Intyre (eds.), *New Essays in Philosophical Theology* (The Macmillan Company, 1955). The contributors to the latter volume are about equally divided between Christians and non-Christians, and this balance is reflected in the case of the editors who are also evenly divided in this regard.

10. Milič Čapek, " The Development of Reichenbach's Epistemology," *The Review of Metaphysics,* XI (1958), p. 67.

11. Susanne K. Langer, *Philosophy in a New Key* (Harvard University Press, 1942). A more recent edition is available (1951), and the book has recently appeared in paperback. A third edition was published by Harvard University Press in 1957.

12. Ludwig Wittgenstein, *Tractatus Logico-Philosophicus* (Kegan Paul, Trench & Co., London, 1922). This work forms a kind of watershed for the logical thinking of linguistic analysts.

13. Langer, *op. cit.* (1951 ed.), p. xii.

14. Paul Tillich, " Religious Symbols and Our Knowledge of God." *The Christian Scholar,* XXXVIII(1955), p. 189.

15. W. Köhler, *Gestalt Psychology: An Introduction to New Concepts in Modern Psychology* (Liveright Publishing Corporation, 2d ed., 1947), pp. 3–33.

16. Jacob Bronowski, " Science as Foresight," *What Is Science?* edited by James R. Newman (Simon and Schuster, Inc., 1955), p. 435.

17. Immanuel Kant, *Critique of Pure Reason,* translated by N. K. Smith (The Macmillan Company, London, 1929), p. 504.

18. This suggestion is made by William Barrett, " Existence and Analytic Philosophers," *Irrational Man* (Doubleday & Co., Inc., 1958), pp. 262–271. The essay, appended to his book by Mr. Barrett, is an interesting and provocative comparison of two modern directions in philosophic thought.

19. John B. Carroll, *The Study of Language* (Harvard University Press, 1953). An invaluable bibliography is appended to this study, pp. 246–268.

20. Otto Jespersen, *Language: Its Nature, Development and Origin* (The Macmillan Company, 1922), p. 64.

21. Cf. F. S. C. Northrup, *The Meeting of East and West* (The Macmillan Company, 1946), pp. 430 f.

22. An excellent summary discussion of the dimensions of lin-

guistic science is provided by S. Ullmann, *The Principles of Semantics* (Basil Blackwell & Mott, Ltd., Oxford, 2d ed., 1957), pp. 1–42.

23. Langer, *op. cit.*, p. 68.

24. Aristotle, *Organon, de Interpretatione* 2 (translation my own).

25. Gaston Paris, *Journal des Savants* (February, 1887), p. 65.

26. C. K. Ogden and I. A. Richards, *The Meaning of Meaning* (Harcourt, Brace and Company, Inc., 1925), pp. 272–304.

27. *Ibid.*, p. 14.

28. Charles Morris, "Foundations of a Theory of Signs," *International Encyclopedia of Unified Science*, Vol. I, No. 2 (University of Chicago Press, 1938), pp. 6–42.

29. Alfred Korzybski, *Science and Sanity: An Introduction to Non-Aristotelian Systems and General Semantics* (Science Press, Inc., 1933). This book is now in its fourth edition (International Non-Aristotelian Library Publishing Co., 1958).

30. Korzybski, "Outline of General Semantics," *General Semantics*, edited by Hansell Brough (Arrow Editions, 1938), p. 1.

31. Anatol Rapoport, *Operational Philosophy: Integrating Knowledge and Action* (Harper & Brothers, 1953), p. 19.

32. "*Nectimus nodos et ambiguam significationem verbis inligamus ac deinde dissolvimus.*" Seneca, *Ad Lucilium epistulae morales* xlv. 5 (translation my own).

33. Ullmann, *op cit.*, p. 261; cf. F. de Saussure, *Course in General Linguistics*, translated by Wade Baskin (Philosophical Library, Inc., 1959), pp. 7–20.

34. *Ibid.*, p. 28.

35. Rapoport, *op. cit.*, p. 13.

36. Cf. David G. Mandelbaum (ed.), *Selected Writings of Edward Sapir in Language, Culture, and Personality* (University of California Press, 1949), p. 162. The same section will be found in D. G. Mandelbaum (ed.), *Edward Sapir, Culture, Language, and Personality: Selected Essays* (University of California Press, 1956), pp. 68 f. This essay was written in 1929. Two years later, the same idea was expressed by Edward Sapir, "Conceptual Categories in Primitive Languages," *Science*, LXXIV (1931), p. 578. The notion was also developed by B. L. Whorf, *Papers on Metalinguistics* (Department of State, Foreign Service Institute, Washington, D.C.,

1952), pp. 4 f. These collected papers gather together Whorf's contributions to this particular aspect of linguistic science; they reward diligent reading.

37. Harry Hoijer, "The Sapir-Whorf Hypothesis," *Language in Culture*, edited by Harry Hoijer (University of Chicago Press, 1954), pp. 92 f.

38. *The Book of Common Prayer* of the Protestant Episcopal Church in the United States of America (Harper & Brothers, 1944), p. 32.

39. Jespersen, *The Philosophy of Grammar* (Henry Holt & Co., Inc., 1924), p. 52; the whole section (pp. 53–55) expands this critique.

40. It is self-evident that this question is part of a much larger problem involving the total relationship presumed to exist between language and logic. For a number of years, this problem has occupied British philosophers as is evidenced by two collections of essays: A. G. N. Flew (ed.), *Essays on Logic and Language* (Philosophical Library, Inc., 1951); A. G. N. Flew (ed.), *Logic and Language* (Second Series) (Philosophical Library, Inc., 1953). These essays are a good background for the more strictly theological discussions that have centered on Oxford. Linguistic scientists have leaned more toward anthropology in the American scene, but there is one competent linguistic critique of the problem of language and logic: V. Brøndal, "Langage et logique," *Essais de linguistique générale* (Copenhagen, 1943), pp. 49–71.

41. Geddes MacGregor, *Introduction to Religious Philosophy* (Houghton Mifflin Company, 1959), pp. 269 ff.

42. R. G. Collingwood, *The Idea of History*, edited by T. M. Knox, Galaxy Books, 1 (Oxford University Press, 1956), p. 15 (italics his own).

43. *Ibid.*, p. 17.

44. Langer, *op. cit.*, p. 169.

45. *Ibid.*, p. 180.

46. Alan Richardson, *A Preface to Bible Study* (The Westminster Press, 1944), p. 179.

47. C. A. Simpson, "The Book of Genesis," *The Interpreter's Bible* (Abingdon Press, 1952), 1, pp. 441–450, 491 f.; cf. pp. 195 f.

48. *Ibid.*, pp. 466–468.

49. C. H. Dodd, *The Apostolic Preaching and Its Development* (Harper & Brothers, 1944), pp. 7–33.

50. Ludwig Koehler, *Lexicon in Veteris Testamenti Libros* (E. J. Brill, Leiden, 1953), p. 369.

51. Cf. L. S. Thornton, *Revelation and the Modern World* (The Dacre Press, London, 1950), pp. 163–190, *et passim*.

52. H. Reichenbach, *Elements of Symbolic Logic* (The Macmillan Company, 1947), pp. 1 f.

53. Bertrand Russell, *The Scientific Outlook* (The Free Press, 1931), pp. 71–84. Although somewhat acrimonious at times, Russell's criticisms of scientists as well as humanists always seem to touch the heart of the matter.

54. That this is Wittgenstein's primary contribution to the development of philosophic thought is adumbrated by I. A. Richards, hinted by Anatol Rapoport, all but explicitly stated by Susanne Langer, and cogently argued in one of a series of incisive essays by Margaret Masterman in *Theology*, LIV (1951), pp. 51–58.

55. Max Knoll, "Transformations of Science in Our Age," *Man and Time: Papers from the Eranos Yearbooks*, edited by Joseph Campbell (Routledge & Kegan Paul, Ltd., London, 1958), p. 266. This whole essay is a perceptive study of the alteration of stance in modern scientific research.

56. In the terminology of linguistic science, a *linguist* is a practitioner of linguistic science, a linguistic scientist; a *polyglot* is a person proficient in the use of several tongues, usually living tongues. Cf. Carroll, *op. cit.*, pp. 1 f.

57. See, for example, the way in which this question underlies the presentation of Greek philosophy in W. T. Jones, *A History of Western Philosophy* (Harcourt, Brace and Company, Inc., 1952), pp. 3–91.

58. In the Masoretic text, this is v. 5; the translation is my own.

59. In this book (Longmans, Green & Co., Inc., 1943) and in its successor, *Existence and Analogy: A Sequel to "He Who Is"* (Longmans, Green & Co., Inc., 1949), Dr. Mascall's orientation is frankly Thomistic; the kind of Thomism for which he contends seems, however, to be difficult to achieve. As the preface to the second work indicates clearly, Mascall is to be considered Neo-Thomist

in the best sense of the term (cf. *Existence and Analogy,* pp. xvi–xix).

60. Originally conceived as the Annual Mid-Winter Lectures at the Austin Presbyterian Theological Seminary in 1951, this work achieved publication as number 8 in the series Studies in Biblical Theology (Henry Regnery Company, 1952). The preface to this study is a succinct and coherent statement of the nature of what has come to be known as Biblical theology (pp. 11–13).

61. The way in which the two parts of this book fit together, despite the fact that they were written independently, is a reflection of the unity that peculiarly pertains to the Bible for all of its diversity. This work is a part of the Christian Faith Series, Reinhold Niebuhr, Consulting Editor (Doubleday & Co., Inc., 1957).

62. This observation is not intended to convey the impression that Barth is unaware of the necessity to translate; instead, it is intended to underline Barth's appreciation of this necessity. The author finds himself in agreement with Tillich at this point, for Tillich is careful to grant Barth's intention while criticizing the way in which he carries out the intention (cf. Paul Tillich, *Systematic Theology* [University of Chicago Press, 1951–   ] I, pp. 4–5, 7–8). Barth sets forth his own conception of the task of translation in his *Church Dogmatics* (*The Doctrine of the Word of God,* Vol. I, Part I, pp. 433 f.; Vol. I, Part II, pp. 620–622). Since selection was necessary, if the present study was to remain within reasonable bounds, and since Barth's position has been examined in detail in various current studies, the author has chosen to omit further analysis of the *Church Dogmatics* in favor of a more thorough discussion of other representatives of the translation enterprise.

63. Paul Tillich, *Systematic Theology* I, pp. 3–8.

64. Cf. Noah E. Fehl, " A Case for Systematic Theology," *Anglican Theological Review,* XLI (1959), pp. 23–35.

65. It is impossible to interpret otherwise the words — " *Quod theologiam illam sua auctoritate tantopere comprobat* " — of the encyclical letter *Humani Generis* (August 12, 1950). An official English translation of the encyclical letter in its relevant parts is to be found in *The Sources of Catholic Dogma,* translated by Roy J. Deferrari from the 30th edition of Henry Denzinger's *Enchiridion Symbolorum* (B. Herder Book Company, 1957), p. 639, No. 2313.

66. Cf. H. J. Blackham, *Six Existentialist Thinkers* (Routledge & Kegan Paul, Ltd., London, 1952), p. 78. It is interesting to speculate upon whether or not the promulgation of *Humani Generis* was in any way responsible for Marcel's repudiation of the label of " Christian existentialist "; cf. Gabriel Marcel, *Metaphysical Journal*, translated by Bernard Wall (Rockliff Publishing Corporation, Ltd., London, 1952), pp. xii f.

67. Peter Alexander, " The Difficulties Which the Scientist Experiences in Accepting Theological Statements," *The Christian Scholar*, XXXVIII (1955), pp. 206–218.

68. A. D. Kelley, " A Functionalist Approach to Christology," *Anglican Theological Review*, XXXIII (1951), p. 12.

69. Bernard E. Meland, *Faith and Culture* (Oxford University Press, 1953), pp. 57–60, *et passim*. Cf. W. N. Pittenger, *Theology and Reality: Essays in Restatement* (The Seabury Press, Inc., 1955), pp. 61–75.

70. Hans Werner Bartsch (ed.), *Kerygma and Myth: A Theological Debate*, translated by Reginald H. Fuller (S.P.C.K., London, 1953), pp. 1–44.

71. *Ibid.*, pp. 12-15.

72. Noah E. Fehl, *op. cit.*, p. 32.

73. Bartsch (ed.), *op. cit.*, p. 27.

74. Hans Jonas, *Die mythologische Gnosis* (*Gnosis und spätantiker Geist*, I) (Vandenhoeck & Ruprecht, Göttingen, 1934). The first half of the second part, *Von der Mythologie zur mystischen Philosophie* (Vandenhoeck & Ruprecht, Göttingen, 1954), appeared simultaneously with a second edition of the first part. The reader who desires to get the flavor of Jonas can do so without recourse to the German; his recent American publication contains much of the material in the first part of the German work (Hans Jonas, *The Gnostic Religion* [The Beacon Press, Inc., 1958]).

75. Bartsch (ed.), *op. cit.*, p. 24. In place of Professor Fuller's translation of *Dasein*, " the ontological structure of being," we should prefer either to translate " existence " or to leave the word in German. Professor Fuller's translation seems to say more than Bultmann means by *Dasein*, although it is an accurate rendering of the word as Heidegger means it.

76. M. Heidegger, *Sein und Zeit* (Max Niemayer, Halle, 4te

Aufl., 1935), pp. 41, 234 f., 2–8, 15–19; cf. Paul Tillich, *Theology of Culture*, edited by R. C. Kimball (Oxford University Press, 1959), p. 95.

77. Götz Harbsmeier, " Mythos und Offenbarung," *Kerygma und Mythos*, edited by H. W. Bartsch (Herbert Reich, Hamburg, 1948), pp. 49–73.

78. Cf. Hendrik Kraemer, *The Christian Message in a Non-Christian World* (Kregel Publications, 3d ed., 1956), p. 292.

79. A. D. Kelley, " The Interpretation of the Christian Faith," *Anglican Theological Review*, XXXVI (1954), p. 7. The entire article (pp. 3–11) is *multum in parvo*.

80. Tillich, *Systematic Theology*, I, pp. 28–46.

81. *Ibid.*, I, p. 49.

82. *Ibid.*, I, pp. 10–12.

83. Nels F. S. Ferré, " Tillich's Philosophical Theology," *Scottish Journal of Theology*, X (1957), p. 237.

84. Tillich, *Systematic Theology*, I, p. 263.

85. B. E. Meland, *Faith and Culture*, is a stimulating presentation of the viewpoint of *process theology*, and it deals responsibly with the problems inherent in translating the Christian faith into viable contemporary terms. An informative bibliographic footnote (pp. v f.) specifically refers to other representatives of this school of thought. A brief, but no less comprehensive, statement of Dr. Meland's position in *Faith and Culture* will be found in his "Interpreting the Christian Faith Within a Philosophical Framework," *Journal of Religion*, XXXIII (1953), pp. 87–102.

86. B. M. Loomer, " Neo-Naturalism and Neo-Orthodoxy," *Journal of Religion*, XXVIII (1948), pp. 79–91; " Christian Faith and Process Philosophy," *Journal of Religion*, XXIX (1949), pp. 181–203. These two essays delineate Dr. Loomer's position with reference to process thought and Christian theology; they indicate the lines along which he should contribute to the production of a systematic theology in terms of process philosophy. Equally illuminating is his critique of Tillich's thought in " Tillich's Theology of Correlation," *Journal of Religion*, XXXVI (1956), pp. 150–156.

87. D. D. Williams, *God's Grace and Man's Hope* (Harper & Brothers, 1949); like Meland, *op. cit.*, this work reaches toward a systematic treatment, even if only within the scope of a single topic.

Cf. also his *What Present-Day Theologians Are Thinking* (Harper & Brothers, 1952), pp. 58–61, *et passim*.

88. The indebtedness to the essay of B. M. Loomer, " Christian Faith and Process Philosophy," is evident throughout this paragraph; the writer gratefully acknowledges the helpful insights gained from the essay and personal conversations with Dr. Loomer.

89. The best and most readable edition of this work is *Origen: Contra Celsum,* translated with an introduction and notes by Henry Chadwick (Cambridge University Press, Cambridge, 1953).

Index